THE INNER PATH
in Universal Life

Level of Order

THE
INNER PATH
in Universal Life

Level of Order

Revealed
by Brother Emanuel,
the cherub of divine Wisdom,
given and explained through the
Prophetess of God

Gabriele - Würzburg

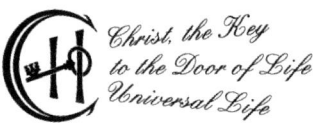

Second Edition 2006

Published by:
© Universal Life
The Inner Religion
PO Box 3549
Woodbridge, CT 06525
U S A

Licensed edition
translated from the original German title:
"Die Urchristliche Lebensschule. Der Innere Weg zur
Einswerdung mit dem Geist Gottes in Uns.
Level of Order"

From the Universal Life Series
with the consent of
© Verlag DAS WORT GmbH
Max-Braun-Strasse 2
97828 Marktheidenfeld/Altfeld
Germany

Order No. S 121en
The German edition is the work of reference for all
questions regarding the meaning of the contents

All rights reserved

ISBN 978-1-890841-41-6
ISBN 1-890841-40-4

The correct use of these schooling texts

In the "world," we have our classes of instruction and schooling and it goes without saying that an elementary school pupil cannot attend a higher grade level right away. The same holds true for the Inner Path.

If we want to skip some "classes" of this schooling or want to follow or try out several paths at the same time, we will be torn in our thoughts and actions and will no longer know what is right and what is wrong.

When we have no goal before us, we feel torn. This inner conflict leads to tension and disturbs our inner balance.

For this reason, our advise is to take seriously the schooling presented here and follow only one path – which path is left up to the individual!

The path offered here is a gift of our Redeemer, Christ.

One can walk it or not. However, if a person does follow this path, he should concentrate totally on this one path, and free himself completely from side paths.

The Original Christians in Universal Life,
followers of Jesus of Nazareth

Table of Contents

Foreword *11*

The Inner Path to the Heart of God *13*
Christ-revelation from April 18, 1987
Revelation from Brother Emanuel Oct. 18, 1991

Important Notes to Consider *18*

1. Initiation *23*
Prerequisites for the Inner Path – A calling? – Heroic sacrificial courage – From without to within – Right discipline: Love for God – Hearing voices – The inner word and the prophetic word – The purification of the soul

2. Basic Teachings and Instructions for the Level of Order *50*
Upon awakening – The soul prayer – The sun prayer – The right discipline and alignment – The mystical journal – The evening – Remarks

3. Body Rhythm and Training the Organ of Sight *79*
Discipline – The first task: body rhythm – Order of thoughts – Refinement of the senses – The second task: Training the organ of sight by contemplating a plant – The meaning of the soul

prayer – The greeting of peace – The effect of negative thoughts – Summary

4. Lessons on Sight and Hearing, and Overcoming the Past 107

Everything is a revelation of God – God is the love – Recognizing correspondences – Exercises for training the eyes to foster the consciousness of unity: contemplating minerals and stones; contemplating animals; contemplating nature – From training the senses to schooling the heart – The origin of thought – Memories and correspondences – Vagabond thoughts and ever-recurring thoughts – Letting the past rest – Forgiving and asking for forgiveness – A lesson on hearing: The effect of disharmonious and harmonious sounds on the body rhythm – Wisdom – Encouragement by Brother Emanuel – Summary: A good foundation; a step-by-step refinement instead of castigation; consciousness, subconscious, soul – From the human to the spiritual; repetition of the tasks

5. Self-recognition by Training the Senses of Hearing, Smell and Taste 154

Development of the senses and order of thoughts – Fight before the victory – The divine in all things – Man as sender and receiver – Task: Alternately turning the sense of hearing to within and to without – Training the senses of smell and taste (inner and outer days) – Conscious eating and uncontrolled food intake – Fulfilling desires – Planning – Letting go and living in the present – The "gliding" soul prayer – Love for neighbor – The satan of the senses – Aging and inner youth – Inner freedom and inner peace – Summary

6. Training of the Sense of Touch 198
The uncontrolled sense of touch – Seven-times-seven aspects of consciousness – The person as the plaything of his outer senses – Everything is vibration – The person as the target of different forces – Exercise: conscious touching; alternating outer and inner days – An upright cast of mind and an upright physical posture – Excessive gesticulation and harmonious posture – Exercise: an "excursion" into the cosmos – Communication with the beautiful, positive forces in everything – Questions for men and women (the second mask, the beard and long hair, clothing) – "Sense of humor," clothing and celebrations of love in the spiritual world – Summary

Self-examination for Proceeding to the Level of Will 237

Glossary of Spiritual Terms
Books to order 241

Foreword

We are on earth to become divine again!

In our time, Christ has again called a Christian Mystery School into being. In this high schooling of the Spirit, His servant, the cherub of divine Wisdom called Brother Emanuel on earth, teaches the direct and shortest path to God by way of the prophetic word.

The prophetess of God, our sister Gabriele, walked this steep and direct path to God ahead of us. It is the path of purification, the path to the cosmic consciousness, to the conscious unity with God. By walking this path before us, our sister had to experience and suffer through much. This is why she can understand us in everything and help us in our development – on our own path to the eternal, heavenly homeland.

The basic instructions in this book are from the revelations of our spiritual teacher, Brother Emanuel. Through the opened spiritual consciousness of our sister, we receive practical instructions and specific exercises on the level of Order, which help us to actualize the deep spiritual knowledge that the Spirit of God reveals to us in our daily life and to become free from the ballast of our human ego.

On the first level of the Inner Path, the level of Order, we learn to put our thoughts in order, to curb our speech and to refine our senses and turn them inward. The motto is: Recognize yourself! This means to recognize and overcome all weaknesses, inclinations, bindings, opinions and conceptions – by turning them over to Christ and no longer doing the negative things we have recognized. On this tightrope path we fight our human ego, our faults and our selfishness, not through fanaticism, but out of love for God. By repenting, forgiving and asking for forgiveness, and through the transforming power of Christ, we become free step by step for a life of peace with our neighbor.

Through self-recognition and the actualization of the eternal laws, soul and person can spiritually grow. The person striving toward God who completely orients himself to the Highest develops in himself, step by step, the true, selfless love. Through this, he gradually awakens in the divine consciousness to the extent that he opens the levels of consciousness in himself.

The Inner Path to God can be walked by anyone – either alone with this book or in community. In community, the pilgrims on their path to God help each other to recognize themselves to lawfully clear up their faults and weaknesses, their difficulties and problems.

This divine gift is offered to every willing person who wants to walk this Christian mystical path of love to God. And each one can decide freely. However, he should really decide, and then follow this path wholeheartedly, out of love for God. For, we are on earth to become divine.

The Original Christians in Universal Life

The Inner Path,
the Path to the Heart of God

In a great revelation on April 18, 1987, Christ spoke about the Inner Path:

The Inner Path is the path to the heart of God.

Everyone begins by monitoring his thoughts. Oppose human, negative thoughts – thoughts of hatred, envy, animosity, discord, strife – with positive thoughts, thoughts of selfless love, thoughts of peace, hope, confidence and faith. Then the sullen, doubtful, spiteful and derogatory thoughts will fade away. You receive much more light through the positive thoughts, and then it is possible for you to recognize everything that is active in your consciousness and subconscious, perhaps the past, and overcome it by the power of inner love. Your worldly desires no longer compel your senses outward. You will fulfill your smaller desires as fitting to your present situation, and take pleasure in them. In this way, willfulness also subsides, and this willfulness, this base little ego, is replaced by the divine will, which says: "The Father's will shall be done. Father, show me what is good!"

And the One who dwells in you and constantly knocks at your door will, by way of sensations and feelings, reveal to you what His will is. Suddenly you will feel: "Why should I be hostile toward my neighbor? I will take the first step now; I will go to him and ask for forgiveness, even though I thought until now that he should come to me and ask for forgiveness." You take the first step and then feel a sense of freedom. You have let go. The Father in you guided you, and now you feel peace and you emanate this peace. Your neighbor toward whom you harbored animosity is now consciously your brother, your friend.

This encouragement from your inner being brings about further steps. You clear up your past; you let go of what you had bound yourself to, for example, that your neighbor should think and act as you want. Free will says: Your neighbor is just as much a child of God and simply burdened differently. He still has to take this or that step in order to find the path, the direct path, to the heart of God. This was the will of God in you. Let go and be a friend and brother to your neighbor, be a sister, be a child of God, and you will let go, realizing: "Yes, he or she has free will. I may not compel my neighbor or force my will on him."

If you follow the fine sensations of your inner being, then the selfless, impersonal love will awaken more and more in you and you will feel peace and joy. You will feel free and deeply fulfilled; it is the light of the Father in Me, the Christ. Your consciousness expands and you see the world with totally different eyes. You feel that the world needs liberation and that so many people live in the chains of their human ego, enslaved by it. You see need, illness, infirmity and much more. What do you do?

You feel the will of God, a gentle urging in you, which wants to tell you: "My child, take the next step toward divine wisdom, toward the divine deed. Bring justice into this world, for justice shall prevail over right. In this justice, all people and beings who feel God in themselves are united ." You take the first step; and the deed, the wisdom, awakens in you. God, the divine, flows into your sensations and feelings. It wants to say to you: Oh see, the eternal law of love says: Pray and work. The right work is like the right prayer, it is a lawful life ...

You suddenly realize that the Inner Path, the path to the heart of God, is not meant just for the individual, not just for your own unfoldment. On the level of Wisdom, of the deed, you feel that now, you may draw from your inner being; yes, you can do it; you have experience in overcoming your human ego. And you feel the urge to help the inner kingdom grow and develop externally, the inner kingdom to which you are so close.

*The Inner Path,
the Path of Liberation, Is Joy*

On October 18, 1991, Brother Emanuel, the cherub of divine Wisdom, gave us, through the prophetic word of our sister Gabriele, a revelation about the Inner Path. He said:

"Recognize and feel that there is a need for the Inner Path, particularly during this materialistic time. The Inner Path is the path of liberation from the burdens lying on the soul ... And so, you walk this path selflessly — this means that the love for the Father is essential for becoming free from the burdens, for growing closer to God, our eternal Father – then you will also progress on the Inner Path, step by step."

"Oh realize, the Inner Path means to recognize yourself and, with Christ, to clear up your sinfulness, so that you may grow ever closer to the Eternal, to the inner light. And so, the Inner Path is a school of life, in which each student recognizes himself. Self-recognition is necessary; for only if the student recognizes his faults – that is, what is sinful in him – and follows the path of heartfelt remorse, of asking for forgiveness, of forgiving, of making amends and then of no longer committing the fault, that is, the sin that he has recognized, only then is the soul cleansed."

"Behold: This earth is truly the school for the children of God. It becomes much easier for the person who goes to this inner school, because he relieves his soul of the human ego. Gradually he eliminates his egoism. The light of Christ shines more intensely in his soul. The light of the Lord then has an effect in and on his physical body. The person feels better and better, because all is well with his soul, being enveloped and absorbed by the light of love. For soul and person have turned toward the light and have entered the light, which liberates, which shines, which is the path.

Yes, Christ is the way, the truth and the life. No one comes to the Father — but through His Son, Christ, the Redeemer of all souls and men."

"Christ wants to go with you, for you have chosen Him. Choose Him anew each day, and you will recognize that the Inner Path is joy. The Inner Path is liberation and happiness; yes, the soul begins to breathe again, for it feels the breath of the Almighty. It feels that it belongs to the kingdom of love, and it wants the person to truly become an instrument of love."

Important Notes to Consider When Beginning the Level of Order

At the beginning of the level of Order on the Inner Path, we remind you once more of the prerequisites for walking the Inner Path in Universal Life. We ask you to pay attention to the following:

Dear brother, dear sister, when you decide to walk this intensive path in Universal Life, you should feel an inner readiness to consistently align your life with the master in you, with Christ.

You should do no other spiritual exercises or practices beside this intensive course, even if they are called Christian.

Let us imagine that we want to cross a river. The river is our human ego which needs to be overcome. If we enter two boats by putting one foot in each boat, we will falter with the slightest current, and a stronger current will cause us to totter and fall into the water. This is also the case on the Inner Path: When we cannot clearly decide for one spiritual path – in our picture, for one stable boat, which we believe will take us safely to the other shore – we will be shipwrecked sooner or later.

Every person is at the same time a transmitter and a receiver. When we orient ourselves toward several vibrations by practicing different spiritual techniques at the same time, a whirl of forces will become effective in us, in the receiver, which not every person can withstand.

The schoolings on the Inner Path in Universal Life are directed to spirit, soul and body. They can lead to impairment in people who:

– are suffering from mental disturbances or illness,

– have undergone psychiatric and / psysychotherapeutic treatment during the past three years,

– take mind-altering medications, sedatives or stimulants (like, for instance, Valium, Librium, Lexotanil, antidepressants, neuroleptics, amphetamines, sleeping pills and so on),

– are dependent on narcotics and drugs (including alcohol and nicotine),

– engage in spiritual practices or techniques (such as Yoga, Zen, TM, autogenic training, etc.) or have done so until recently.

The course should be interrupted during pregnancy. The expectant mother carrying the growing embryo should not be exposed to any great fluctuations of the human ego, so that the embryo can calmly prepare itself for the incarnating soul.

After birth, the course can be continued where it was left off. However, it is advantageous to repeat the last step or steps.

Dear sister, dear brother, the one who sets out on the intensive path of schooling should no longer be struggling with very severe problems with his fellow man, particularly in marriage and partnership. He should have mastered his past to a large extent, that is, he should have above all forgiven and asked for forgiveness wherever there was strife with his neighbor.

He will then no longer dwell on the past in his thoughts, but will start each day alert and concentrated. He will use the energies given to him by God with purpose in accomplishing the daily exercises and tasks. Through steady work on himself, he will grow spiritually and expand his consciousness. Thus, the Inner Path will bring him joy and inner fulfillment.

Dear sister, dear brother, the first level on the Inner Path, the level of Order, consists of a revelation of initiation as well as five consecutive chapters with teachings and lessons, which help us walk the Inner Path successfully.

The tasks and exercises described in the second chapter "Fundamental Teachings and Instructions for the Level of Order," are the foundation for the level of Order and are practiced during the entire course. The tasks and exercises described in the subsequent chapters 3 to 6 should be practiced until you feel that you have actualized them for the most part. Only when you have completed all the tasks of one part should you proceed to the following part, since each part is based on the preceding one.

And so, dear sister, dear brother, you can see that the pilgrim on the Inner Path determines his own progress. However, this requires a certain degree of self-discipline and honesty with oneself.

From our experience, we know that we fall when we try to take the second step before the first one. The same applies to the Inner Path: When we go to a new task, without having actualized the previous ones for the most part in our everyday life, we will fall. But if we are honest with ourselves, the Inner Path will give us much joy, and we will experience harmony in us.

Greetings in God!
The Original Christians in Universal Life,
followers of Jesus of Nazareth

1. Initiation

*Prerequisites for the Inner Path – A calling? –
Heroic sacrificial courage – From without to within – Right
discipline: Love for God – Hearing voices – The inner word
and the prophetic word – The purification of the soul*

—

*Our sister Gabriele greeted us
as students on the path to God:*

*Greetings in God dear brother, dear sister!
The first hour that leads a willing person striving toward God onto the Inner Path to the Kingdom of God in us is an initiation from the Spirit of the Lord.*

We received the following instructions in the Christian Mystery School, the high schooling of the Spirit of God on earth, through Brother Emanuel, the cherub of divine Wisdom and a law-angel. These instructions are for all people who want to ennoble their senses in order to grow nearer to the divine in a human being.

On the first four basic levels, from divine Order through divine Earnestness, the schooling and ensuing actualization brings about the cleansing of the soul and the expansion of consciousness, so that at the end of the fourth level we are able to hear Christ, the almighty power in the Father, in us. We will not experience this great mystery until our consciousness has attained the necessary expansion through the cleansing of our soul.

The Spirit in the soul reveals itself to the one who has dedicated his life, all his thinking and striving, to Him, the great All-One. Then he will see people and things as they really are.

To hear the Spirit within us is only a preliminary step toward our unity with the eternal Being. In the end, we should once again be as God created us. Then we will no longer need to listen within, instead we will be ourselves the universal consciousness again.

The universal consciousness is the logos in us, the Spirit, which then senses, thinks and speaks through us. We will no longer be dependent on human words that actually say so little, and that often deceive and confuse the one who only listens to the word and does not grasp the meaning. The enlightened one who has found his way out of the wheel of reincarnation no longer takes what is said as fact. Instead, he sees behind the words, because he knows a person as he is – as he thinks and lives, not as he pretends to be. The veils that had clouded our senses have fallen from us. Because of this, we see our neighbor as he really is, not as he pretends to be.

A further development of our consciousness brings the inner vision, an eye for what is spiritually noble and beautiful. Taken all together, a life out of the eternal law is the highest mystery that a person can attain at the end of the Inner Path.

In order to reach this high goal, the pilgrim on the path within first has to crucify his human nature, his ego. Through self-recognition and actualization, he has to grow and mature spiritually. This means that only through the actualization of the eternal laws can soul and man attain the high goal.

Dear brother, dear sister, you are now putting your spiritual foot onto the Inner Path. Before we begin with the initiation for the level of Order and with the first lessons and exercises, I ask you to heed the following:

The Inner Path is a tightrope walk. On this straight and narrow pathway, our ego, all our humanness, will come to meet us in many shapes and forms. Our past will rise up in us. Things and events that we had long forgotten and not thought about will take hold of us again, because they still lie in our soul and surround us as radiation. They are those things that we still have to work on, or events for which we should ask forgiveness or forgive.

On the Inner Path many things will come our way that concern solely ourselves. This is why this path is called the path of self-recognition and actualization of God's laws – so that we become divine again.

But without spiritual knowledge we cannot walk the path within to the Kingdom of God. And without Christ, our Redeemer, we will not progress. Through His sacri-

fice on the cross, Christ gave us the power to return to the Father-house. His help and support are the grace on our way there.

However, we have to take the first step on the path within: We have to recognize our faults and weaknesses, the burdens of our soul and body, and we have to try to gradually discard them. Then the grace of the Eternal in Christ will become increasingly effective in us. For His Redeemer-deed is balm and strengthening for our soul.

Since Christ's Redeemer-deed, there is no longer a way back to the Absoluteness without Christ. For this reason, the Inner Path is possible only with Christ. The redeeming grace of the Lord strengthens us and helps us to overcome everything that hinders us from becoming the image of God again. But we have to do our part, in order to advance lawfully on the Inner Path. We should fight our ego – not through fanaticism, but out of love for God – and bring it to Christ, who is then, with us, the conqueror of our burdens.

Human beings have been given a mind. If it is schooled accordingly – that is, if we are understanding and loving toward our neighbor, without immediately judging or condemning him because his opinion is not ours or because he does not do what we want – then reason prevails over intellect, which is limiting and likes to teach lessons to its fellow man and belittle him.

Therefore, let reason prevail! Reason tells us that those who begin to walk the Inner Path should not be satisfied with half-measures. It would be a half-measure to believe that within a short period of time on the Inner Path, we would be far enough along to be able to hear the voice of the Eternal and to see the heavenly worlds and their inhabitants. Self-recognition pulls the reasonable person back, over and over again, when he begins to think that he has already gone far on the spiritual path. Reason lets him see where he stands and with what kind of thoughts he surrounds himself, thoughts that beguile him, so to speak. The one who is true to himself, by not fooling himself, will very quickly recognize his spiritual state and will realize that he often fools himself and that his desire was the father of his thought.

Wanting things is very dangerous on the spiritual path. When we want something, we send out thoughts that work for us. The more often we send our desires into the world, the stronger these thought-complexes become. Our desires then work for us as thought-complexes, providing us with those things that we had sent out as wishful thoughts.

For instance, if we want to come into contact with cosmic inhabitants, with souls, then this can happen if we think we must collect inner experiences by any means. Astral experiences, that is, perceptions from the soul realms of the purification planes, are not inner experiences. They are not based on our inner devel-

opment, but are brought about by our wishful thoughts, which have built themselves up externally in the form of force fields.

Such and similar wishful thoughts are dangerous on the Inner Path. Not only can they deceive our senses about reality, but then can also call up forces which then influence us so strongly that we no longer are in command of our senses. Therefore, let reason prevail!

We want to please God, by putting our thoughts and senses in order and by purifying them. We are children of the All-Highest and we should be inspired only by the one wish to please God, our Lord and Father, in striving for a life in accordance with the divine laws.

The Inner Path offered in Universal Life is not for making contact with entities from the in-between realms, nor for gaining particular perceptions through the utmost human effort of will. The Inner Path in Universal Life is a schooling, in which the alignment of soul and person with the highest goal is striven for: to become divine again, that is, to think, speak and act in a noble, pure and good way.

Our sensations should be the same as our thoughts, and our thoughts should be the same as our words and actions. When we can speak everything that we think, without hurting our fellow man, we have reached a high degree of selfless love. Then we can say that we have successfully taken some steps on the Inner Path.

The Inner Path in Universal Life can be seen as follows: We now step into an elevator without windows. On the level of Order, we press the fourth button. It is the fourth basic level of consciousness, the divine Earnestness, where the Redeemer-light is burning.

We will strive to master our life, not in idleness, or in a reclusive existence, or even through castigation, but by self-recognition and by overcoming what we have recognized as negative in us. We surrender our ego to Christ, our Redeemer, who guides us on the Inner Path with His grace and love.

We will not be driven by self-love and curiosity to stop the elevator and look out to see what is happening in the in-between realms. And so, we will not interrupt our journey to the Kingdom of God out of curiosity, in order to see what life is like in the still-existing realms of shadows. Thus, we will not stop the elevator by pushing the first or second button in order to look out on the level of Order or the level of Will, so that we can see what goes on there, in the in-between spheres.

We strive to direct our eyes to the <u>one</u> goal: to become free from our base nature, from our ego, which torments us and wants to seduce us with human thoughts again and again. And so, we remain in the elevator, without asking what it is like in the astral spheres. Nor will we emit our human desires because we want to hear something. For when we want something, we will receive it, according to our wanting and our desires.

If we remain steadfast despite the tightrope walk, despite the ups and downs, our efforts will be richly rewarded. Once we are cleansed and purified and have completed the fourth basic level for the most part, the divine sets in as if automatically: We become the divine law again, and the law, God in Christ, then manifests itself to us.

The only desire we should cherish and nurture is to become divine again, pure, noble and good in our sensations, thoughts, words and actions, in everything we do.

Dear brother, dear sister, the Inner Path in Universal Life is a gift from God, our Father, in Christ, our Redeemer. We may accept His gift thankfully. But we do not have to accept it, we may!

Note well: Every one of us has free will. No one is forced to believe what is revealed, or to walk the Inner Path. What God, our Lord in Christ, our Redeemer, offers in His work, in Universal Life – His word, the path – is absolutely free.

Dear brother, dear sister, you can walk the Inner Path or leave it. We will not influence any brother or sister. God has given free will to every person. We respect this. However, as brothers and sisters in Universal Life, we have one request: Should you walk the Inner Path in Universal Life, then do it with your whole heart! Do not follow other spiritual paths on the side! Decide either for this path or for another one. You are free to choose which one. But, we ask you to make a choice and to decide, so that in the course of your spiritual development, you do not run into difficulties in relation to this.

If we want to walk two paths, sooner or later they will cross. Every time these two paths cross, you will have personal problems. Either you will grow tired, because it is far more difficult to walk two paths than one, or you will have difficulties with your faith. You will have doubts as to which path is the right one. The reason for this is that you have walked neither one of the two paths correctly, from within.

For this reason, we ask you to examine and think about which path you want to follow. If you walk the Inner Path in Universal Life conscientiously, with reason and the right decision, then you will feel joy on the path within.

Every brother and sister begins the initiation of the level of Order with lessons and exercises. The brothers and sisters of Universal Life wish you spiritual success. We accompany you on the path within, in love and gratitude toward God in Christ, who has given us this direct path to the heart of God, our eternal Father.

The light of the Godhead radiates to us from the eternal Being. It gives us peace and harmony. We may feel the love of our eternal Father through Christ, our Redeemer.

Dear sister, dear brother in the Lord, may you, too, be touched by this eternal power!

The love, the light, our homeland, wants to guide us more and more. On the path of love we are guided by Brother Emanuel, the cherub of divine Wisdom, one of the seven law-angels.

Dear brothers and sisters, we see this hour in the Spirit as an hour of peace, in the exalted feeling that God, the all-power, is close to every one of us who sincerely and honestly wants to walk this path to the eternal love.

In 1985 Brother Emanuel
said the following to the intensive students,
which is also valid for you,
dear brothers and sisters on the Inner Path. He said:

Many of you are weighing whether the path of love for God may be the right one, whether you really are properly prepared for the Inner Path and whether you meet its requirements.

Friends, every soul is <u>called</u> through the Redemption of Christ. <u>Chosen</u> are those souls and people who align their life seriously and consciously with God, the inner wellspring, by actualizing the holy laws. If the path of love is walked consciously and oriented toward the goal, but without fanaticism, then the student is <u>chosen</u>.

Therefore, dear sister, dear brother, examine yourself, whether or not you are willing to wade through and explore the highs and lows of your human ego, so that you can grow toward the divine goal through self-recognition and actualization.

The path of love is the path of journeying within to the kingdom of the inner being. Love is the highest source in the universe.

During the schooling Gabriele said:

The love of God is very near to every one of us. It is the incorruptible power of our soul. On the Inner Path, we may activate this power and thus grow closer to our eternal homeland, from where we once came.

The more of our human ego we vanquish, the stronger the power of love in us becomes, and the more radiant, shining and selfless we become. Through this, we find our way to our inner homeland, to the peace and love, which this world cannot give us.

Dear brothers and sisters, we may therefore ask ourselves: Why are we impelled to walk the Inner Path to the Kingdom of God? Why do we want to let go of our humanness in order to gain the spiritual?

Our soul senses the cosmic life. It has awakened and feels that it is not of this world. It longs more and more for its true homeland, for its land of origin. It longs for purity and for peace, which exists only in another world, in the absolute Being.

If our soul had not heard the call of the Infinite and if we had not been inspired by the one desire, to become free from our ego, from our base nature, we would not follow the Inner Path. We would continue to be unawakened people in the din and turmoil of this world.

But the imprisoned soul, entangled in the human ego, heard the call of the Godhead. The person, our outer garment, felt and sensed the call of the Almighty and let himself be guided by the inner force of the soul. And so, guided by the inner love, by this awakening impulse of the soul or by the impulse of an already alert soul, the person began to seek. The awakened and urging soul, filled by the inner longing to return to its origin, touched the garment, the person. The person began to search and finally, often after many detours, found the spiritual wealth that corresponded and corresponds to him.

Dear sister, dear brother, we are called to unfold the inner love, the selfless love, the love for God. This requires heroic sacrificial courage. We have to fight our base nature in order to finally vanquish our self.

However, Christ is the victor with and in us. He gives us His light, His peace and His love. God sent His Son, so that He lead us back to the heart of God, our Father, who wants to have us with Him in the light of truth – as His conscious images.

On the path within, we have to recognize our self-made hurdles and overcome them through the power of love. We have to recognize them, so that we no longer fall back into the same faults and weaknesses, into one and the same burden. This is why there are the familiar fluctuations on the path within. Highs and lows have to be experienced and overcome, so that we attain constancy, the steadfast harmony in God.

We will experience many things on the Inner Path. We will proceed with single-minded determination, and then again experience stagnation when we think about our past over and over again – when we brood about our experiences and cannot forgive our neighbor or ask him for forgiveness.

We will also find that we will have to awaken our love for the Infinite time and again, because we fall into half-heartedness over and over again and let our mind be clouded by our senses.

But the one who always gets up and is willing to make sacrifices on the path within will proceed victoriously.

On the Inner Path "through self-recognition to the experience of God," we will have to recognize that, unfortunately, we preoccupy ourselves most of the time with our base ego – with our "mine" and "yours," "this belongs to me and that to you," and "I am my own best friend." Yet, the one who takes the Inner Path seriously and is thankful each day for his self-recognition and for the strength to actualize the holy laws will find out that God calls him at every moment.

And so, to overcome ourselves and to get up and begin again over and over, truly means to have heroic sacrificial courage. But what does heroic sacrificial courage mean?

A person has to struggle with himself by the day, by the hour. Only through the willingness and courage to make sacrifices can we vanquish our base ego. Only this brings soul and man closer to the love of the Father. Only by sacrificing our human inclinations and drives will our soul become the image of our Father again.

Heroic sacrificial courage also means to have the courage to recognize yourself! Have courage and take the sword of selfless love! With it, sever the many heads of the snake: self-love, egocentricity, envy, hatred, desire and passion!

Nevertheless, we should remember not to castigate our body, but to <u>gradually</u> overcome our humanness, bit by bit. If we do not castigate ourselves, that is, if we do not deny ourselves everything from one day to the next, thus entering a life of privation, we will make progress on the Inner Path. But if we castigate ourselves, if we deprive ourselves overnight of many things, we will tire on the path within and suffer stagnation, or even give up the path altogether.

The transformation from the base to the higher, going all the way to the Absolute, has to take place slowly.

Many people think that when they walk the Inner Path, they have to give up all things external from one day to the next. They think they are not allowed to eat this or that any longer and that they must let go of this or that. Here, I am also referring to our professions, our jobs. But no, it is not so. The external is transformed through the inner being.

A prerequisite on the path within is that we first put our thoughts in order, that we curb our speech and gradually master our senses. What good does it do to pretend to be pious? If we deny ourselves this or that, thus tormenting ourselves by depriving ourselves of these things?

So let us begin by putting our thoughts in order! If we ennoble our thinking, much will change, also externally, as if automatically.

On the first level to perfection the motto is: Put your life in order! Put order in your life, in your thoughts, words and deeds!

For us to stabilize on the level of divine Order, discipline and alignment are necessary. We will practice the right kind of discipline only when we have a deep love for God, when we love God, our Father, more than the pleasures of this world, and even more than our past that keeps coming up in the present, occupying our thoughts.

On the Inner Path, it is important to clearly know what we want: whether or not we want to master our past, which is often a great hindrance on the path to perfection. If we have put our past in order for the most part and strive to live in the present, we will also understand the lessons and tasks from the Spirit of love and will actualize them joyfully.

To attain a certain degree of alignment on the first levels toward perfection, it is necessary that we repeatedly take ourselves back, because a person turns to without very quickly. His senses are quickly in the world again, and he finds his way back into his inner being only with great difficulty.

This is why Brother Emanuel, our spiritual guide, gave us the soul prayer, which we do three times a day. Its effect is to draw back our senses, which are used to living in the world, over and over again. Through the soul prayer, we attain an ever deeper alignment with our inner being and, in the further course of the Inner Path, with the life in our inner being.

In order to do the soul prayer three times a day, we need the right kind of discipline and love for the Eternal.

In 1985, Brother Emanuel revealed the following basic thoughts to the intensive students:

Without love for God, our Father, there is no real discipline and, without love and discipline, there is no path!

Those who believe that they can walk this path without love for God and neighbor and without the right discipline will fail on the path within.

Many dangers lurk for those who walk the Inner Path only out of curiosity, who do not have the right love for the divine.

The one who daily strives to sacrifice his ego, who surrenders his base nature bit by bit to Christ, also leaving it in His light, will feel in himself the stream of divine love and the help on the path within.

But the one who walks this path half-heartedly will have nothing but difficulties, with himself and with his neighbor, since he lacks love and alignment.

Brother Emanuel also spoke
about hearing voices:

Hearing voices can be very dangerous, particularly to those who want to thereby exalt themselves and be important. The curiosity to experience things from the world of the spirits, no matter from which spheres, to hear or receive answers to questions, is dangerous! These desires should be put aside on the path within.

On the path of divine love, we are called to purify the soul, to ennoble soul and person in sensations, thoughts, words, actions and gestures, so as to actualize higher ideals and values in this way – thus attaining the alignment with God in Christ, who wants to be our leader.

Mankind is in a great turn of time: The primordial power and the part-power (the Redeemer-power) are bringing about the guidance of all souls and men toward higher spirituality. The primordial power in particular induces the cleansing of the earth, bringing the planet earth into higher vibration. Through this, the power of God streams ever more strongly into the material and part-material spheres, and into the purification planes. All men and souls are being grasped, more or less strongly, by the primordial power and the Redeemer-power, according to their spiritual alignment.

Just as the light of God is growing ever stronger on this earth, with the same intensity, the adversary is beginning to mobilize his own. This means that bound souls are increasingly pressing toward the earth, to influence <u>those</u> people who live on the same wavelength as they.

Furthermore, souls that live in the lower spheres of the worlds beyond are seeking to incarnate, in order to live on earth once more as they conceived it while in the earthly garment and as they continue to imagine it in the beyond. Their conception presses them to incarnate and also to manifest, through people, those things that they would like to see realized in the world, namely, their own conceptions.

Hearing voices is a result of what is taking place in the spheres of purification as well as on earth. If a person is receptive, that is, sensitive, it is possible that he may receive and carry out impulses from one or several of these senders.

Our sister Gabriele said:

Again and again the Spirit of God is asked the question: Where do the impulses come from, or is it the inner word, the word of Christ?

Brother Emanuel gave us the following answer:

Dear friends, may each one examine himself, may each one think about himself:
Where are your thoughts on a daily basis?
In what world of thoughts do you live?
What preoccupies you day by day?
How big is your individual person, still?
Is every other thought truly a God-thought already, a thought of selfless love?
What do your inclinations, your desires and your longings still consist of?
What burdens you day by day?
What do your ever-recurring and tormenting thoughts consist of?
Do you live in strife, in animosity, with your neighbor?
Are you still spiteful toward your neighbor? Do you hate?
How do you live in your family? Is everything going well? Is there quarreling and fighting? What is the reason?

The person to whom these questions apply fully or even partially can be sure that he summons astral influences by wanting to hear voices. Depending on the intensity of the different sources and the sensitivity of the receiver, they will then become active in the person. This is not the inner word! They are inspirations from various sources, which the person calls up according to his way of thinking and living.

The one who in his inner being has largely purified the first four soul garments – from the consciousness center of Order to the Christ-consciousness, the level of divine Earnestness – that is, who has imbued them with light, is secure in himself and can receive impulses from the Godhead. However, these impulses are meant for him, not for a second or third party. Impulses from the pure source do not say: You have to do this and must not do that. They only give advice, for God gave us free will. He does not boss us around.

But the person who wavers in his life – torn by human inclinations, base thoughts and desires, then again deeply moved by a shallow longing for the voice of the Almighty – does not live in God. He also cannot hear the voice of the Eternal with this.

So, based on these questions, whoever can say with a clear conscience: "I have overcome everything human for the most part, my four soul garments are filled with light" can perceive impulses from the eternal source. But these are meant for him personally, not for a second or third party.

The person who has incarnated from the divine spheres with a mission to pass on the voice of God to others has at his side a control being, a teacher, as it were, who also assumes the function of protecting the speaking instrument. The control being guides the streams of the Almighty that flow from the soul to the brain cells, so that in the brain only <u>those</u> cells are touched that put the eternal truth in the right words, so that the person can understand the stream of God in his mother tongue.

The one who has not incarnated with a spiritual mission, but claims to be a speaking instrument of the Most High, through whom God teaches second and third persons, does not have a control spirit at his side. According to the law of the Almighty, he may not pass on to a second or third party the impulses that were meant for him, even when the impulses are reformulated in his brain cells and expressed as if they were intended for others. Such a reformulation in the brain, in which the stream of God seems to express itself as if the revealed were meant for a second or third party, takes place because there is no precise alignment in the brain of the receiver.

A control being has an essential function with a speaking instrument who has been called for a divine mission. It is responsible before God that the speaking instrument live in accordance with the laws of God and totally subject his human will to the will of God. If an instrument with a mission follows human ways, despite the admonishments and instructions from the control being, then the control being will respect free will and gradually discontinue its function of spiritual control.

The purity of the instrument is important for the transmission of the pure word.

*Our sister, Gabriele,
gave further suggestions about this:*

If in our sensations and thoughts we are not pure for the most part, then we will merely draw on the mixed good from our inner being and pass these on. The person who receives the mixed good and passes it on is responsible for doing this, not the person who hears the mixed good from the other, who believes he is hearing the voice. Whoever is satisfied with the mixed good cannot follow the Inner Path of purification, the path of love for God.

May each one now rate himself: What do I prefer? To draw from the pure wellspring or to receive from different spheres of life, from different astral sources?

Gabriele continued:

Dear sister, dear brother, the path of love for God lies before us. We have to decide whether or not we want to subordinate our willing to the will of God.

So that the will of God can become effective, we need to put order in our thoughts, to curb our speech and to align our senses. On the level of Order, we want to very deliberately examine and train these three forces: order, speech and the alignment of our senses.

The law of our heavenly Father does not want us to castigate ourselves as pilgrims on the path to our eternal homeland.

Especially on the path to God, many different kinds of difficulties will come up again and again. We should master them gradually with great sacrificial courage, with joy and, above all, with love for God.

The highs and lows on the Inner Path are the movements in our life. They are good and very effective for soul and person. Only they make it possible for us to recognize ourselves as we are. From them, we can see the humanness that still clings to us and what we have to surrender, so that we can advance on the Inner Path by actualizing the holy laws.

There are ups and downs on the path to God. These lead to decisive effects in our life. The consciousness and the subconscious of a person are addressed in this process; whereby much will come up which we believe to have already overcome, but which merely lie repressed in the subconscious. Through self-recognition and surrender to the Eternal, these areas of our consciousness are purified. In this way, the person becomes more free and peaceful.

The one who overcomes the valleys of his consciousness and subconscious will break through to his soul garments, which we have to purify as well, in order to gradually draw closer to the goal.

Without the redemption through Christ, we could not reach our goal. Christ is the redeeming and liberating Spirit in every soul. Without Him, there is no path to the heart of God! Jesus said: "No one comes to the Father but through Me."

Brother Emanuel
gave us further essential suggestions:

The Inner Path, the Christian mystical path, is the path of love. On the level of Order which you now enter, dear brother, dear sister, the following should be remembered:

You are now walking the path of love for God and for your neighbor. The person who wants to actualize in himself the love of the Father, the power of the soul, more and more, should master his problems.
Whoever does not master them, but lets them be, will have nothing but problems on the path within. For if mere knowledge is accumulated and nothing is actualized, there will not only be stagnation in the development of soul and body, but a revolution that may lead to illness and great suffering.

Gabriele said:

This is why those of us who are a step ahead of you on the path to God give warning: The person who only accumulates knowledge and does not actualize is afflicted and tormented by his own problems, which may cause illness and great sorrow.

We all know that not every problem can be surrendered to Christ from one day to the next. We have to tackle the greater problems over and over again, and cut off a piece of it again and again and give it over to Christ. Of course this is a struggle with ourselves. But when we tackle the problem and if we want to overcome it, then Christ, our Redeemer, also stands by us. Having overcome it, we feel like a newborn. We have been delivered of something dark, and light streams toward us.

Problems develop through wrong thinking and acting, through egocentric feeling, thinking and speaking.

Through wrong, egocentric thinking, self-pity, too, develops. This, in turn, has its side effects like, for instance, aggression and depression.

When we do not want to work on our problems, when we only speak about them, we will increase our problems. The consequence is that they affect us more and more. The results are self-pity, aggression, depression and the belief that our neighbor does not understand.

We know from experience that not every problem can be mastered by ourselves. We need the help of those who have experience, who are a step or two ahead of us. This help is given during the discussion hours of the personal courses in the intensive schooling of the Inner Path, in seminars and other meetings. There you will have the opportunity to talk about serious problems, which we will then try to solve together in a lawful way, with the help of the Lord.

We have all had to, and still have to experience that sacrifice and struggle precede victory. Without sacrifice and the fight with ourselves, there is no victory over our base ego!

Dear brother, dear sister, the brothers and sisters of Universal Life ask you to reflect on these words of initiation, and whether you are willing to persistently align your life with the master in you, with Christ, by doing your part, as well, in striving to put your thoughts in order, in curbing your speech and in mastering your senses.

Our spiritual teacher, Brother Emanuel, now gives us the first part of the teaching material for the level of Order. The level of Order should build a good foundation for the following levels. We walk these subsequent levels to gain further recognitions and learn about deeper divine laws and actualize them, so that we reach a fulfilled life, which is the mark of the true mystic.

The brothers and sisters of Universal Life wish you, dear sister, dear brother, much strength and God's blessing! May the strength of the Father in you give you the perseverance to walk the path in love for Him and for your neighbor. This leads to joy and contentment.

Greetings in God,
Gabriele

2. Basic Teachings and Instructions for the Level of Order

Upon awakening – The soul prayer – The sun prayer – The right discipline and alignment – The mystical journal – The evening – Remarks

—

Our sister, Gabriele, addressed the students on the Inner Path with the following words:

Greetings in God, dear brother, dear sister! We now receive the first lessons from our spiritual teacher, Brother Emanuel.

He said:

My friends, on the level of Order we practice monitoring our thoughts. What is a positive thought, what is a negative thought? What effect does a positive thought have on soul and person? What effect does a negative thought have on mind and body?

Furthermore, on the level of Order, I teach that a person should pay attention to his words: to what he expresses and to what he wants to put into his words. Why should the student pay attention to his words? Why should he speak only essential things and surrender everything unessential to the Eternal?

Another subject is the alignment of the five senses. But first comes the soul prayer, which helps us to turn within.

The soul prayer prepares soul and person for the inner life. It trains and stabilizes the spiritual consciousness. Through the different exercises, the cell structure of the person is gradually purified and the soul is aligned and attuned to the cosmic power, to the inner life.

The alignment and attunement of the soul is more or less difficult for the person, because, in former lives, as well as during this earthly existence, he programmed his soul and his brain cells with externalities, with human inclinations and stirrings.

As long as the consciousness of a person wavers, he is one time world-oriented, then again God-conscious. Therefore, a steadfastness and, at the same time, a change of thinking by turning toward the laws of God must take place. This means that the person learns to feel, think, speak and act more selflessly and divinely.

This reorientation from the human ego to God, to a life willed by God, to the actualization of the laws, causes difficulties on the way – more or less – depending on the soul's burden and on the individual's body of thought.

To lay the foundation for further levels on the level of Order, the brain cells have to become gradually imbued with light. They have to be aligned with a nobler, purer and much nicer way of thinking, with spiritual ethics and morals.

This reorientation does not take place from one day to the next. It may be a long and arduous process, depending on how great the love of the student is for God, his Father.

But the one who strives for self-recognition deliberately and purposefully and who fights his human thoughts, words, stirrings and inclinations, who loves God more than all the existing difficulties and problems, will become master over himself.

Our sister Gabriele said:

The term "soul prayer" expresses that we want to let our soul pray, which is the consciousness that we have opened. This does not mean that the student should do the soul prayer in order to hear a voice or voices.

Brother Emanuel revealed:

However, dear friends, this requires practice and going within, to the inner power.

Every beginning is difficult, also with the soul prayer. May the student want nothing while doing the soul prayer. He should not expect anything. He should do the soul prayer so that his wavering consciousness is stabilized and attains alignment with the divine. This leads the student to the true, deep, selfless prayer, the prayer of the soul.

The soul prayer is a preparation for the true, genuine, inner I Am. It may take years, or even decades, to hear the inner power, the pure I Am, the inner love, depending on the burden of the soul and on whether the soul prayer is done joyfully or whether the student considers it a nuisance and a disagreeable task.

Through a soul prayer done thankfully and joyfully, the person will become more still and find his way to the depths of inner life. Then, the prayer is not produced by his mind. In the course practicing it, it will be the consciousness of person that prays.

I repeat: In the course of time, when the soul has become stabilized and the consciousness has a firm hold in the divine, it will be the soul that prays and not the mind. And so, it is the soul that prays. It is not God who is speaking to you, to instruct you personally!

Brother Emanuel continued to reveal:

In the morning, the pilgrim to the kingdom of the inner being awakens in the awareness of God. This means that his first thought and aspiration is to let his love for the Father become effective in him, by linking with God, his Father, whose Spirit dwells in his soul, immediately upon awakening.

When a person wakes up, his consciousness and subconscious want to become active right away. "Vagabond thoughts" that are buzzing around will try to influence you. And the impressions, desires and longings lying in your consciousness penetrate to you as waves of thought, trying to mentally influence you. This means that you think about everything that should still be, what already is, what was wrong, what is good, what should be done, what has been done, whether what your neighbor or colleague said was right or wrong, which instructions the boss gave that have not yet been carried out, and much more.

To be able to largely withstand these influences, the pilgrim on the path within should link with the eternal power <u>immediately</u> after he awakens, by praying his thankfulness for the night and for the new day <u>into his inner being</u>.

When wishful thoughts, all the not yet done or already done tasks, doubts, discord and the like penetrate to your inner being, command these troublemakers not to influence you. Give yourself the right commands! Then your thoughts will obey you – which, in the end, you have produced yourself, and which are a part of your own nature.

Command your thoughts with the following words:

"May everything that is important and necessary for the day, and which has to be fulfilled and done, touch me when I am ready for it!"

Say this several times and program yourself in this way. By so doing, you will take in what is positive and important, and side issues will be secondary.

Upon awakening, the pilgrim on the path within should link with the inner wellspring, with the love of God. This can be done in the spirit of the following words:

"Father, I thank You for the night.

Kind Father, You have awakened me again for the new day, so that I may accept it and recognize it as a gift of grace from you and put aside the humanness that is still a part of me.

Through your love, I have awakened and have been strengthened anew.

May Your love go with me and guide me throughout the day."

Brother Emanuel continued:

Dear friends, the right discipline is also a sign of our love for God. The right discipline brings reverence and respect for God, for life.

For this reason, the pilgrim on the path within should also give honor to God, the life, in his movements and gestures. For the whole universe is harmony, balanced, rhythmic life. The pilgrim on the path within should join in with this rhythmic, balanced life, the all-harmony of God.

This is why every movement and every gesture is significant. The person has to come into harmony in order to attain harmony in his inner being as well. Positive thinking brings about harmonious movements and balanced gestures, all in all, a harmonious rhythm.

Upon awakening in the morning and while still lying in bed, the pilgrim on the path to God should offer his first impulse of gratitude to Him, the Almighty. The disciplined pilgrim to the inner homeland lies on his back and crosses his hands. The right hand is placed on the chest, with the left hand over the right one. Through this body posture, the eternal wellspring in man, the spirit-power, can flow more intensely.

After this brief, but fervent, heartfelt prayer of thanksgiving, the pilgrim on the path to God gets up harmoniously. Then he does the sun prayer, also called the ether prayer.

He stands facing the east. He lifts his arms, with the palms also facing east. In this prayer position, he addresses the All-Spirit of infinity in the spirit of the following words:

"Eternal stream of infinity,
You, the All-Spirit in all Being!
Fill my soul and my body
with spiritual power,
with Your life.

Eternal Spirit!
Stream through the particles of my soul,
and the cells of my body.
Awaken my whole being

to the conscious, harmonious life
that You are.

Eternal all-harmony!
Flood through my consciousness and subconscious,
purify them with Your almighty power.

Eternal One,
purge and purify my senses, too;
put my life in order,
for may Your will be done."

This sun prayer or ether prayer should stream from the heart and from the soul.

The person who still has the time and opportunity should do the body movements after the sun prayer. Afterward, the pilgrim on the path to God takes his bath or shower and gets ready for the new day.

After dressing, he goes to a quiet room. This room should become a prayer room, a small temple, to which he returns again and again, when he is overcome by restlessness and the like.

If it is possible for you to make such a room available, or even a little, quiet corner, keep this room or corner sacred. Positive vibrations will build up there and when you sit down in this room or quiet corner, they will envelop you and positively attune you.

And now we come to the soul prayer.

The pilgrim on the path to God sits in an upright position, just as he has learned in the Original Christian Development of Consciousness.

An erect sitting posture will benefit the pilgrim not only during the contemplation and soul prayer, but when doing the subsequent exercises.

In the course of the Inner Path, the upright posture, which he gradually becomes accustomed to, helps him to look not only at the ground, but into the far and wide. The result is that the pilgrim on the path to God takes in life in all its diversity and gains a sense of the far-reaching expanse of infinity. This leads to more light-filled thoughts and nobler character traits.

Brother Emanuel said:

My friends, linger in the stillness for a few moments and let your sensations stream up to the core of being of the soul. From your heart, love shall stream forth, which links with the great primordial heart, God, the unending love.

Without thoughts, but with only selfless sensations, the pilgrim lingers in the core of being of the soul, which is located near the pituitary gland.

With his own sensations and words, he now directs a prayer to the eternal power, the Father in Christ, in the following sense. The prayer written below should serve as an aid. However, you should not pray it word for word; instead, your prayer should stream from <u>your</u> world of sensations. The words of this prayer are only a guideline for you:

"Father, You have called me through Your Son.
I, Your child, have heard Your voice.
Lord, my love is still small,
but it is my will to find my way back to the origin.
This is why I will kindle my still small love for
You, so that I may become again
what I was and am in Your Spirit –
an absolute being of infinity.

I bring my small love to You.
I place it on the inner altar.
In addition, I place everything that separates me
from You, the great love, on the inner altar,
so that Your flame may leap up
and nourish the small flame of love in me,
so that I become again the great flame,
the luminous power from Your Spirit."

The love-sensations of the child for the Father now stream to the consciousness of Mercy. Having arrived there in his sensations, the pilgrim on the path to the Kingdom of God again prays the following brief prayer:

"Eternal source of power of Mercy!
Once I left the eternally holy stream;
I went through the gateway, into the depths
and became a human being.

Again and again, love was the driving force in me.
It knocked at the gate of my heart,
but I did not hear it.
Now, I have heard the awakening call of love.
Now, I feel You,
O eternal source of power of Mercy.
Now, it is evident to me
that I can completely open again
the eternal source of power of Mercy –
through Christ, my Redeemer."

Vivified by the inner love for God, the pilgrim goes on to the consciousness sphere of the level of divine Love, which lies between the eyebrows as a source of power. There he prays with his sensations:

"Eternal consciousness,
I have enveloped you with my ego.
I dissolve these garments
through the power of Christ in me.
Purified, I return
to the consciousness of Love.
Love is my eternal being.
I will be love again,
through Christ, who has called me."

With his inner sensations of love, the pilgrim goes on to the next level of consciousness, Patience, which is anchored in the neck region as a source of power.

He prays with words like the following:

"Eternal Patience,
you source of power from the stream of God!
Once I left you,
and enveloped this radiant field of eternal Being.
Now I am called to imbue these garments
with light
through the redemption of my soul,
through Christ in me.
Now the source of power called Patience
opens up again.
I come back from the depths of my human ego,
and rise to the wellsprings of the eternal Being,
to the origin of love.
This is to where my path leads me."

Now the pilgrim lets his love-sensations stream to the consciousness level, the source of power of Earnestness, which is effective between the shoulder blades.

There, he prays in turn with words like the following:

"Christ,
You, in the consciousness of Earnestness!
Through the eternal love for the Father,
through discipline and alignment,
I now awaken
the eternal source of love in me.

Lord and God,
I ask You for guidance.
Christ,
lead me to the origin of the source,
to divine salvation.
You are in me, and I am in You.
Lord, let everything become
as it was and is from the very
primordial beginning.
Christ, my Redeemer,
vivify me;
strengthen me on the way to the Father."

More love-sensations of the pilgrim now stream to the consciousness of divine Wisdom, which is effective near the lumbar region.

"Lord and God,
I have acquired lawful knowledge,
but I still lack Your divine wisdom.
I have recognized that knowledge alone
does not awaken Your forces in me.
Only Your wisdom shows me who I am
and where I stand.
It reveals to me all things of life.
I have recognized
that despite spiritual knowledge, I am still deaf,
burdened by my human ego.

For this reason, O eternal love and wisdom,
I immerse in the holy consciousness
of divine wisdom,
and actualize the knowledge that has been
offered to me,
so that I may become wise,
in the spirit of divine love and wisdom.
I return again to the heart of the Father,
through Christ, my Redeemer."

More love-sensations of the pilgrim now stream to the divine Will, to the source of power located in the sacral region.

With words similar to those that follow, the pilgrim prays:

"Father,
my ego – all my willing, thinking and striving –
still torments me.
My ego and the 'my' and 'me'
do not want to let go of me.
But it shall get better with me!
Yes, I want to fulfill Your will completely.
With heroic sacrificial courage,
I fight my willing,
so that Your will may enter me,
and that, from now on, I fulfill Your will alone!
Then I will become free from my base nature,

and will rise to Your divine wellspring,
from where I went forth –
from Your love."

Now, your love sensations stream to the divine Order, to the source of power, which is effective in the coccyx region:

"Eternal Father in Christ,
I am still on the level of Order.
But Your Spirit in Christ guides me upward
to the origin of love,
from where I went into the depths.
I have shadowed myself,
but now I am becoming more and more light-filled,
until I am again light of Your light."

Below the source of power of Order is the spiritual collective basin, where the energies gather, the forces that come from the incorruptible core of being. By way of the force-fields of Mercy, Love, Patience, Earnestness, Wisdom, Will and Order, they stream down into the collective basin. From there, they flow back again to the incorruptible core of being of the soul. While doing this, they vivify our physical body by way of the nervous system.

And so, the forces flow upward to the region of Order.

"Holy Order,
help me put my thoughts in order,

to curb my speech
and master my senses!"

With his sensations, the pilgrim to the kingdom of the inner being is now in the center of Order. He concentrates all his attention on this center.

He now switches to "receiving." This is possible when all thoughts are turned off. Almost automatically, selfless prayer-thoughts now rise, which are either grasped mentally or expressed verbally, depending on what is possible for the student. This is the soul prayer.

In the beginning, this brief soul prayer lasts a few minutes at the most, because the student is not yet able to concentrate deeply.

Afterward, the student goes upward again with his sensations to the primordial source, to the core of being of the soul. In so doing, the pilgrim prays again on each level, by going upward with forces of love:

"The holy powers of Will will vivify me,
so that my willing subsides
and the will of God becomes effective in me.

Divine Wisdom touch me!
Knowledge is not wisdom.
Divine wisdom, however,
beholds all things in the right light."

With his sensations, the pilgrim on the path within now goes to the consciousness of Earnestness and prays a brief prayer using words like the following:

"Christ,
You, the pulling and pushing power in me!
You lead me out of my narrow,
self-centered thinking
and guide me to the source of love."

In his sensations, the pilgrim now goes to the consciousness levels of Patience, Love and Mercy.

At each level, he prays respectively, using words similar to the following:

"O stream of Patience,
take hold of me!

Compassionate Love,
penetrate me!

Eternal Mercy,
let me become a selfless samaritan!"

The pilgrim goes with his sensations to the core of being of the soul, using words to the following effect:

"Father,
I thank you for joy and sorrow.
You great All-One are closer to me

than my breath.
Lord, the day now begins for me.
O eternal One,
I place this day, which is Your day,
and myself, too, into Your kind hands."

After a brief reflective moment of stillness – harmoniously aligned with the inner source – the day now begins with breakfast, work, and so on.

Brother Emanuel
gave further tasks to the pilgrim on the path
to the kingdom of the inner being:

Dear friends, in the course of the morning, you will be faced with unrest and haste again and again.

Whatever comes toward a person from without and moves him is still partly alive in him.

This could be desires or worries, but also thoughts about your neighbor or about one of your colleagues at work. In addition, the hectic activity of your neighbor that makes you feel unsettled results in some things coming into movement in your inner being. These are not the divine, the calm and the peace, but are human aspects that become active in your soul and in your soul garments.

They are often only remnants of the human ego – inner functions that also become active in the consciousness and the subconscious.

The pilgrim should not immediately analyze this restlessness and hectic activity that touch him and stimulate him accordingly. Instead, he should first counter with determination these unlawful forces stimulating him to become hectic and restless. Using the following words, he addresses his inner restlessness and hectic nature:

"I live in Christ.
I work through Christ.
May everything that is not in Christ
go to Christ,
so that He transform it!
My thoughts and desires, my conceptions
and worries, I consistently surrender to Christ.
Christ accepts everything.
I give it up to You, O eternal Spirit in me!
Joyfully and thankfully,
I place it at Your feet
and try to leave it with You, as well.

Calm, deep calm, draws into
my consciousness again.
I am calm and still, concentrated on my work,
without asking my ego if it agrees with the
determined way with which I oppose it."

Brother Emanuel continued:

However, the pilgrim shall record what he cannot deal with – what shows up in his sensations and thoughts over and over again, what keeps flooding through him: thoughts, desires, conceptions, a hectic activity and restlessness – in a book that we call the mystical journal.

Every pilgrim on the path within starts keeping such a personal mystical journal.

On the right side of this book, the student writes down the positive thoughts, the deep, vivifying and quickening thoughts and sensations, the stillness of his being, which he feels, and everything that he was able to overcome in the name of Christ.

On the left side, he records what still hinders him from growing closer to the inner life: These are, for example, the problems that he could not yet overcome despite his heroic sacrificial courage, all the ever-recurring difficulties that he placed before Christ, but that nevertheless keep coming back, making him feel unsettled despite his efforts. The pilgrim records all this on the left side of his mystical journal.

These notes are made late in the morning as well as in the late afternoon. They show the pilgrim what he has overcome and what he has not yet overcome.

He then crosses out whatever he has overcome; what he has not yet overcome he underlines, and on the following day he carries it over to the next page of his mystical journal, until it, too, can be crossed out because it has been overcome.

Around noon, if possible before lunch, the pilgrim should do another brief soul prayer. By doing the soul prayer, he achieves alignment with his inner being once again. Through this, he regains the calm and peace that he lost during the morning.

And so, the midday soul prayer is done like in the morning soul prayer, but much more briefly:

The pilgrim to the kingdom of the inner being glides down to the collective basin with some highly vibrating prayer words and then lets the forces stream up to the center of Order. There, he switches to "receiving" and lets it pray. Then, with some words of love, he glides upward in his sensations once again to the core of being of the soul and thanks the Almighty, lingering in the stillness for a few moments or minutes. Now the afternoon can begin.

The afternoon should again be under the control of the pilgrim. He should endeavor to keep calm in all things and to cultivate the stillness of his heart.

This does not mean that the person becomes lazy and thinks that he should do everything in a slow meditative way. The one who has awakened the Spirit in himself is dynamic and harmonious. He will do his work in a balanced and harmonious rhythm, concentrated on the task at hand to the satisfaction of all around him. God is harmonious dynamism, harmonious rhythm.

Either in the course of the afternoon or in the evening, the pilgrim will record the positive as well as the negative experiences in his mystical journal. Please note the occurrences and train of thought only in outline form! The mystical journal should be clearly laid out!

Brother Emanuel continued to reveal:

Dear friends, whoever returns from his daily work in the evening should not go to the dinner table immediately. Go into stillness first! Let everything in you subside, everything that the day brought you and made you feel unsettled, restless. Reflect on yourself briefly:

Take your mystical journal and examine it. Whatever unlawfulness you were able to overcome by the evening can be crossed out. Whatever was not overcome is underlined and transferred to the next page of the journal, so that it is not lost, and the pilgrim is reminded over and over again of what still needs to be put aside. Rejoice in the positive side, in what you have overcome! Let it resound in you once again and be glad, with sincere heart, for what now lies behind you.

Think over your day; let it pass by you once again. Ask yourself what you could have done better and what was good.

Let me repeat, so that you will not forget: Rejoice in what you were able to overcome. Be happy about it! But do not be sad about what has not been overcome. Meet it again with the willingness and courage to make sacrifices, in the name of Christ, and it will become in each one of you. For Christ is the victor in the person of willing heart. With Christ, he will resurrect and go to the Father.

After dinner, the evening begins. The soul prayer should also be done in the evening again. This brings about a renewed alignment of the soul for the night.

Either at sunset or after sunset, when the atmosphere has become still and people are more calm, the soul prayer should be done again. When I mention sunset, this is to say that it depends on the season.

What is important is that you do your soul prayer when the atmosphere has become still, when people have withdrawn to their homes and prepare for sleep. So, the time for the soul prayer can be planned for between 9:00 P.M. and 10:30 P.M., depending on the time of the year.

The soul prayer is again done as it was revealed for the morning, but using other words, which should stream from the being of the student, the pilgrim. It should not be a recited prayer, but sensations from the heart. This is why the prayer – that is, the prayer sensations – is left to the individual.

After the soul prayer – depending on when it was done – the evening can be continued.

At bedtime, align again with the inner light. Lying in bed, thank God, your Father, once more for the day, for everything, be it joy or sorrow. Again, surrender everything to Him in prayer, He, the great All-One, who is the day, even during the night.

A reverent posture while praying in bed is done as I have already revealed:

The person striving toward God lies on his back. He places his right hand on his chest, on the fourth consciousness center, and his left hand on the right one. Then he links with the eternal Spirit in his soul and in every cell of his body – and gives thanks.

Since many a pilgrim on the Inner Path still needs a support for his prayer, I give you the following prayer for the night. However, it should not be prayed literally, but should serve only as guidance and suggestion for all those who still find it difficult to pray freely.

"Eternal One in Christ,
I thank You for this day,
which has come to an end.

Lord,
You have led me and guided me.
I thank you.
You guide every single one,
because You are the impersonal love.
You do not look at our faults and weaknesses.
You see us perfect, O eternal Spirit.

I place all people and all beings
into Your great eternal consciousness,

into Your love.
Eternal One, hold Your hands in blessing
over all brothers and sisters,
over the sick and the needy,
over the hungry and the lonely.
Radiate Your light
to the older brothers and sisters,
and support the youth with Your power,
so that they, too, become as You want,
for they are the coming generation.

Lord,
now the little brother of death,
sleep, enters my consciousness.

Into Your kind and eternal hands,
I commend my spirit,
my soul and my body.

Lord,
Your will be done,
in me, in my soul,
also during the night."

Dear pilgrim, after this prayer of thanksgiving, do not take in any worldly thoughts! May sleep enter now, the little brother of death. You are resting in God and God is effective in you.

Brother Emanuel explained:

My friends, this is the beginning of the Inner Path.

The effort to constantly align with the eternal wellspring, with the love, is the path of love, the mysticism of love for the one who truly honors God in his thoughts, words and deeds, who loves God more than his base ego. He is the one who truly makes progress on the path to God, our Father.

Every day, Christ draws nearer to the pilgrim who is truly willing to make sacrifices, who faces his base ego with courage, surrendering it to the eternal love.

My friends, Christ is here!

The Father has called you through Him. He is your Redeemer. He paves the way for you.

Christ, your Redeemer, wants to lead you to the Father. I, Brother Emanuel, may be your teacher.

May the pilgrim to the kingdom of the inner being not look to the teacher, not attune himself to the teacher, but may he align solely with Christ. For Christ is the way. He, the eternal Spirit, is the truth in all Being, in all pure beings, also in me, your brother, called Emanuel on earth.

Christ is the life in every soul, in every person. We all are the life in God. Happy the pilgrim who lets himself be vivified by the inner power! Verily, he will be vivified and filled by the spirit of truth.

God is the truth. I, Brother Emanuel, speak from the truth.

In the name of the Father and the Son, in the name of the eternal power and truth, I give you the blessing.

May there be light in you! May the light of God radiate through each one of you and guide you!

God has called you. Make use of the opportunity to walk the Inner Path now, in the earthly garment! Christ does not want the soul to return over and over again, to incarnate repeatedly anew.

Dear friends, you have heard the call. Make room in you for this time of grace! Let grace prevail in you!

Now is the time and opportunity given to you to release yourselves from the wheel of reincarnation, through a purposeful, conscious life of love. So free yourselves from the wheel of reincarnation, by way of a goal-oriented life aligned with God and in His will!

To hear the call of God is grace. The one who walks the path within earnestly will be filled with the light of God, with His grace.

The blessing power of the Father fills you with wisdom and dynamism.

My friends,
I thank the eternal Spirit that I may teach and serve you.
Your brother in the Spirit of God, Emanuel.

The peace of the Lord is with you.
Amen.

*Our sister, Gabriele, gave us
some additional remarks about this:*

The one who has little or even no love for God lays a poor foundation. He will do the exercises, given by the Spirit for the Inner Path, inadequately and thus not lay the foundation that he needs to be able to build subsequent levels on it. Without love for God, there is no path to God. For God is love!

The Christian Inner Path is not one of castigation. The person on the Inner Path should not repress anything, but should gradually overcome everything negative. Then, all that is human in him will fall away bit by bit, until he can let go from within of all that is transitory.

Obedience to Christ is the actualization of the laws. For this reason, we have to work on ourselves, so that we can actualize and fulfill the laws and thus follow our leader, Christ, our Redeemer.

Our consciousness is the consciousness of the mind. It is what still lies in our memory, what is familiar to us, with which we work daily. The subconscious lies in the deeper layers of the brain. Whatever we have forgotten, but not yet overcome, is stored there.

The soul is the book of life. In it are light and shadow, the sediment of our positive and negative thoughts and deeds. The negative sensations, thoughts and deeds form our correspondences. By way of the seven consciousness centers, the seven garments of the soul, the soul radiates whatever it has stored. Thus, the soul garments reflect whatever light or shadow the soul bears.

Therefore, it is not our mind that tells us who we are, but the radiation of our soul and the rising burdens of our subconscious.

Dear sister, dear brother, the fight with ourselves is given to us until we have conquered our ego.

You are not alone. Many of our brothers and sisters are in this battle with themselves and raise themselves out of this baseness to higher spirituality and to inner peace, which we need so much in this world.

Many are linked with us. In this spiritual communion, we remain the children of God.

Peace

Gabriele

3. Body Rhythm and Training of the Organ of Sight

*Discipline – The first task: body rhythm –
Order of thoughts – Refinement of the senses – The second
task: Training the organ of sight by contemplating a plant –
The meaning of the soul prayer – The greeting of peace –
The effect of negative thoughts – Summary*

———

*Our sister Gabriele greeted us with the words,
dear brother, dear sister, greetings in God!
Then she said:*

The second revelation for the level of Order was given to us by Brother Emanuel on October 13, 1984.

Brother Emanuel addressed us as his students and wished us inner peace, with the following words:

Dear student, the peace and love of the Eternal are with us!

The path to the love of God is a sanctified path. Only the one who truly sanctifies his life more and more, looking ever less to the external, to the world with its stimulations of the senses, can walk this sanctified path.

And so, only <u>the</u> student who puts his thoughts in order, who curbs his speech and gradually masters his senses can walk the path within.

Gabriele explained:

Dear brother, dear sister!
On the Inner Path you have been hearing again and again about the order of thoughts. Utmost discipline is needed to achieve order in your thoughts. For us human beings, the most difficult thing on the path to God is to put order in our thoughts and to align them with the spiritual goal.

The one who has taken some steps on the Inner Path has had to recognize again and again that only the love for God, our Father, and the longing for purity and spirituality enable us to take the steps consciously. The person who loves God, his Father, more than this world and more than himself, than his thinking, willing and doing, is the one who will progress on the spiritual path.

Spiritual discipline is decisive in attaining self-control – control over our person, over our thoughts, words and actions.

Dear brothers and sisters, we have to train ourselves to have a harmonious and balanced body rhythm, so that we can find our way to the stillness and the inner peace, where the love of God is all-encompassingly effective. And so, we have to attune to God, to the central power in our soul, over and over again. We have to surrender our impure sensations and thoughts and our wanting to the Eternal and subject them to His will. Each day, we have to try to allow no impure feelings into our inner being. Generally speaking, this is spiritual discipline.

Dear brother, dear sister, the entire schooling, all instructions and teachings from Brother Emanuel, are directed toward the one goal: to lead the student to inner stillness and to the inner truth.

Especially on the level of Order, we have to strive particularly for alignment. We have to attune to the inner life, to the inner truth, which is found only in the soul of the person. The student has to recognize and actualize ever more from the law of life, the cosmic law, so that he can achieve a true, deep spiritual success on the Inner Path. However, this requires heroic sacrificial courage from each and every one of us, to truly attain alignment with the Highest.

In the second revelation for the level of Order,
Brother Emanuel spoke again and again
about discipline:

Dear students, as a prerequisite and to be able to actualize further schoolings from the Spirit, spiritual discipline and monitoring thoughts are necessary.

Spiritual discipline means to put your life in order, your senses, your thoughts and aspirations. Attain the nobility of your soul, and then your body rhythm will also be harmonious.

Spiritual discipline results in a balanced, harmonious body rhythm. Through this, a hectic and nervous person becomes more still. His movements become more harmonious; his senses become finer.

Our sister Gabriele explained about this:

Dear brother, dear sister, so that we attain this desired monitoring and control of thoughts, we have to practice discipline.

For this reason, the first task for the student on the level of Order is the following:

The pilgrim on the path to the kingdom of the inner being pays attention to his body rhythm.

Everyone shall now try to harmonize himself from without to within. This means that he should pay attention not only to his thoughts, but also to his body movements. And so, we avoid hectic movements. Fast, disharmonious walking leads to outer and inner disharmony.
This does not mean that we should give up a dynamic life, the dynamism of the body or that we should stop being dynamic! Oh no, quite the contrary! We aspire to the inner dynamism, the spiritual dynamism, the noble, rhythmic movements of soul and body. It is not the hectic

and disharmonious, the externally directed activity, or a life under the pressure to succeed that bring success, but the devotion to the divine, to the power that streams through our inner and outer being and that brings clarity into our thinking.

When we become accustomed to walking in an upright and harmonious way, then we will raise our eyes from the ground and look more often into the distance. In time, the effect is that we think more clearly, because the cosmic powers flow increasingly into us.

Through an upright posture, by looking into the distance, and through a life that strives toward God, we participate ever more in the divine works that are in all forms of life.

Gloomy thoughts cling to the ground. Heavy vibrations drag along the ground. Higher forces flow in the vastness of the cosmos.

To the one who strives toward God, even the conscious contemplation of a flower or of a meadow of flowers, the contemplation of trees and bushes, gives inner refreshment and rest, as well as alignment with God, the stillness. The Eternal reveals Himself only in the stillness. We should also contemplate the starry heavens and the sun with its rays.

We take what we are contemplating into ourselves. This brings peace, trust, hope, confidence and, in turn, the alignment with the Highest. We become more still and more God-conscious, because we feel His power and His presence.

This also allows us to experience that noble thoughts, pure words, purged senses and spiritual dynamism enable us to work in a balanced and rhythmic way – which has nothing to do with a meditative attitude at work: It is a working with the inner power, without hectic activity, yet purposefully and in awareness of our goal. The Original Christian Development of Consciousness texts are a spiritual help for the brothers and sisters who prepare for the Inner Path, so that they can fulfill more easily the tasks for the refinement of soul and person.

Our five senses are not individual forces; instead, the one sensory organ affects the other.

To refine our senses, we should also pay attention to our body rhythm while we eat: Eating in an uncontrolled way, chewing or drinking hastily, also leads to disharmony and to without, into the world of the senses. As soon as we become hectic, our body rhythm changes and we pick up our old habits again, like, for instance, the consumption of alcohol or smoking, etc. Furthermore, very hot and very cold drinks have a disturbing effect on the rhythm of the body. They cause a revolution in the nervous system. The nerves become tense; we could say that we shock them. And the tension of the nervous system, in turn, has a disturbing effect upon the whole organism. In the long run, this may lead to serious damage to the organism. It not only makes us hectic and internally agitated, but indisposition and illness can also be the result.

As soon as we get upset, that is, as soon as we become restless, thoughts fly toward us, or occurrences come to mind again, which we thought we had overcome long since. Through our disharmony, we have brought them back and now move them in our thoughts again.

Many thoughts and events would not have to be looked at and analyzed anymore, if we would not touch these vibrating energy-complexes around us again, by lowering our body's vibration. They would dry out gradually, that is, dissolve and be just a memory in us.

If we do not get our body rhythm under control in time and do not transform the rate of vibration of our body higher through positive, affirmative and goal-oriented thoughts, then more and more vagabond thoughts race uncontrolled through our brain. This causes our soul as well as our body to slip into lower zones of vibration, into spheres where totally different sensations and thoughts vibrate and can then gain entry into us.

Thus, we can be influenced by these vibrating thought-complexes, by these thought-waves. A hectic person, a tense nervous system, is then often no longer able to ward off these unlawful thought forces.

If we no longer overcome the thoughts we have sown, they can befall our entire organism and shake it up like a virus. They can act as a trigger for an illness.

The person who does not fight his thoughts in time, by surrendering them to Christ, the Spirit of the soul, over and over again, becomes a prisoner of these vagabond thoughts.

Whoever constantly broods over his past, that is, who nurtures his humanness with the same thoughts over and over again, only intensifies the thought-complex. It will then influence him ever more.

Brother Emanuel admonished us repeatedly to practice discipline. He said:

Without spiritual discipline, the monitoring and control of thoughts is hardly possible. So that soul and person find their way into the spiritual-divine rhythm, the alignment of the five senses is above all necessary. Hearing, seeing, smelling, tasting and touching have to be refined.

Gabriele:

Therefore, the outer senses should be trained and refined, so that they connect with the inner senses, the senses of the soul, more and more. The more the student refines his five outer senses, the nobler his inner attitude becomes and the purer his soul.

And so, we work from without to within. Whatever refines externally awakens in our inner being. In this way, the refined physical senses gain access to the senses of the soul. They connect and then become the spiritual visionary power: The person senses what takes place behind matter. He senses the spiritual. But he also senses the thoughts of people; yes, he perceives and senses behind the mask of his neighbor.

And so, we register the spiritual in this world by way of our refined senses. But the five spiritual senses also feel those things that were veiled by man, that is, his world of thoughts.

And by way of the spiritualized physical senses, the spiritual senses, the senses of the soul, also feel when danger is lurking. Via the refined physical senses, the spiritual senses also feel and sense the illnesses and afflictions in people; they recognize the difficulty and illness not only in their own body, but also in the body of their neighbor.

In order to attain this spiritualization, we have to journey from without to within. This is why we have the path within. And so, spirituality is awakened from without to within and then grows from within to without.

The five senses of the soul are the five spiritual types of atoms that are found in every particle of the soul. The more we refine our sensations, thoughts, words, deeds and our five senses, the more the spiritual senses – the senses of the soul, the spiritual-atomic structure – turn toward the core of being of the soul, the incorruptible primordial principle. The more we refine ourselves, the more accurately we align our soul antenna with the incorruptible core of being in the soul. Therefore, the more we are aligned with God, the more securely our antenna is directed toward the primordial principle, the more divine powers we receive.

And so, we have to first orient and secure our soul antenna to the divine, so that we can hear the Eternal in us.

Toward a better understanding: Our soul consists of trillions and trillions of spiritual particles. In every spiritual particle are the five spiritual types of atoms. All the spiritual atoms within the trillions and trillions of soul-particles form as a whole the antenna to the divine. And so, we should strive to align our antenna to the core of being, the primordial principle, in order to be able to receive the divine word purely and clearly.

Dear brother, dear sister, Brother Emanuel – the spiritual teacher in Universal Life – admonished us to cultivate the love for all forms of life and to become selfless, so that love grow in us more and more. He said once again – and we should note these words in our mystical journal:

Without love for God there is no discipline.

And without discipline, there is no monitoring and controlling of thoughts.

Without discipline and without monitoring and controlling of throughts, there is no alignment of the five senses either.

All human stirrings and inclinations have to be ennobled and transformed, so that we may become conscious images of God again. When we hear about ennoblement and transformation, we may recognize that the Eternal does not want castigation. To ennoble ourselves means that we will not only gain a greater distance from our humanness, but will also refine what clings to us and moves us – be it food from animals, alcohol, tobacco, carnal living and the like.

This means that we will eat meat more consciously and take less of it. We may still consume alcohol and smoke, but we will watch ourselves as we do it and limit their consumption, reducing the amount and frequency. Our sexual life will be ennobled because we see our neighbor as the temple of the Holy Spirit and will then treat him or her accordingly

This ennoblement takes place gradually. The baseness in us will undergo a transformation in the course of time. This means, we surrender to the Eternal the humanness that is still in us. We no longer need these things. Instead, we will attain the spiritual and thus strive toward the high nobility of the soul.

We now come to the second task, to the training of our organ of sight. We will daily endeavor to train our eyes. We will no longer want to see everything the world offers, but only what is still essential. In this way, we attune our organ of sight to the divine wavelength.

Concerning this,
Brother Emanuel revealed the following:

I begin intentionally with the organ of sight, since the eyes particularly have a very strong influence on all other senses.

Dear students, each one of you now has his or her mystical journal. On the right side of the mystical journal, the student records what is positive, everything that he has already overcome for the most part, everything good and noble. On the left side of the mystical journal, the student enters all those sensations, thoughts and stirrings he could not yet overcome, which pull him down again and again, which burden him over and over again and lead him to without, into the world of the senses.

Brother Emanuel continued:

Until now, you have let your eyes roam and have looked at the world with its temptations and occurrences as it offers itself to the worldly person. This shall now change.

The student on the Inner Path will examine himself more and more. Heed the course of your day and watch which things and events you turn to over and over again, which stimulations your eyes follow. Record the "for" and "against" in your mystical journal.

The right side of the mystical journal shows the light-filled sides of the student, what he could overcome for the most part. The student should be glad of this and thank God for His guidance and help. The entries on the left side of the journal are what the student must still overcome.

Brother Emanuel gave us an invaluable sentence, which we record in our mystical journal:

The one who goes to battle against his base ego has Christ consciously at his side, who helps him and gives him His strength to overcome the base.

Gabriele said about this:

And so, dear brother, dear sister, in order to master ourselves, we need heroic sacrificial courage. We will make progress on the Inner Path only if our love for God and for our neighbor grows, because the love for the Eternal makes it possible for us to overcome many things, yes, everything.

Brother Emanuel gave us another task, for training our organ of sight. We go into a contemplation: We look, for example, at an evergreen tree, a flower or a bush, whatever we like at the moment. However, it should be a plant. We look at the object as we have seen it up until now, that is, only as matter. We look at it solely with our physical eyes, only externally, without involving our inner being. We keep our eyes open as we do this. We look at the object. We record our thoughts and feelings in our mystical journal, either on the right side or the left side, depending on the sensations, thoughts and feelings we had.

A little later, we will again look at the same plant or another one. We look at it, but then close our eyes and take the picture, the impression of the plant, into our inner being. There, we let the impression reverberate. We again record in our mystical journal whatever we feel, sense or think while doing this.

We can do these exercises two or three times a day, especially when we suddenly feel that our senses are turning strongly to without and our body rhythm is becoming hectic.

I may repeat: Particularly the training of the organ of sight is of great significance, because it has a very strong influence on the other four senses.

Dear brother, dear sister, I would also like to remind you of the soul prayer.

Strive to practice the prayer of the soul with joy and thankfulness. Particularly the effort to penetrate deeper into the layers of the soul has the effect that we gradually attain the alignment with the Highest.

Let us imagine a well. Pure spring water flows deep in the well, under all the debris of stones and sand. A thirsty person will do his utmost to reach the source. With much effort, yes, with his last ounce of strength, he will clear out the well in order to reach the water, the source.

It is similar with the soul prayer. The more disciplined and joyful we do the soul prayer, the more quickly we find our way to the source, to the inner life. However, all the other tasks that we should do to attain ennoblement of soul and person are also a part of the soul prayer. Only in this way, by refining and spiritualizing our thoughts, words, actions and senses, do we find our way to the pure wellspring.

We also want to think about our greetings: How often is the greeting "good morning" or "good evening" expressed carelessly and without thinking, simply because we are used to it?

Brother Emanuel taught us
the greeting of peace. He said:

The greeting of peace will become a need for the person who feels the peace of God in himself.

Gabriele:

So, when we say the greeting of peace, it should stream from our inner being. What is given out of selflessness produces an echo in our neighbor and in ourselves.

The greeting of peace will become a need of the heart for those who successfully progress on the Inner Path, that is, who ennoble themselves more and more. Spiritual people greet each other from within, from the peace of the soul and of their frame of mind.

We, too, want to cultivate this greeting of peace now. But only the pilgrims on the path within should greet each other with the salutation of peace, without shaking hands. If we want to wish peace to a person of the world, we can do it in our thoughts. But if a brother or sister offers their hand to us and greets us with "good morning" or "hello," then we will also offer our hand and reply with "good morning" or "hello."

We should become free people. The one who actualizes the laws of God becomes free. He will be able to sense into every situation correctly, because he, too, has gone through the levels of humanness and has overcome them through Christ.

Our spiritual teacher, Brother Emanuel, said:

The person who conscientiously strives for actualization, in the right love for his neighbor and for all forms of life, will not castigate himself. Only the one who has actualized little castigates himself. Every castigation makes you unfree and gives rise to obsessions, in which the person who castigates himself believes that his neighbor must think and act as <u>he</u> does.

Every person has free will. Whatever he does, he has to account for before God, not before people. Only the person who actualizes the laws of God will be understanding of his fellow man, since he does not castigate himself, but rather is a conqueror of his human nature.

Gabriele continued:

The greeting of peace should therefore grow from within; it should be a need of our heart.

Brother Emanuel explained to us that every castigation has its offshoots and side effects. What we repress today may show itself tomorrow in a totally different way.

For this reason, it is said on the path of love: Recognize yourself and overcome your ego! Piece by piece and in awareness, conquer what you have recognized as contrary to the law and be thankful to the One who has infinitely much patience with His children: God, our Father in Christ, our Redeemer.

Dear brother, dear sister, let me give you a brief summary of the instructions concerning the teaching material of the second presentation for the level of Order.

Brother Emanuel revealed to us:

The path of love is a sanctified path. Only the one who truly sanctifies his life more and more, who looks less and less to the external, to the world with its stimulations of the senses, can walk this sanctified path.

Gabriele:

Dear brother, dear sister, it is also important for us, who have stepped onto the Inner Path, to know that only <u>that</u> person can walk this path successfully who is willing to put his thoughts in order and to gradually master his senses. I repeat the admonishment of Brother Emanuel once more:

To attain order in one's thoughts, utmost discipline is needed. It is still difficult for many of us to put our thoughts in order and to align them with the spiritual goal, God. This is possible only for the one who loves God, his Father, more than this world and more than himself, than his thinking and wanting.

Our sister Gabriele reminded us:

We have to acquire a harmoniously balanced body rhythm, in order to find our way more and more into the stillness and into the inner peace, in which the love of God is more intensely effective.
The entire spiritual schooling, all instructions from the Spirit, are directed toward the one goal of leading

us to the inner stillness and to the inner truth. Especially on the level of Order, the alignment with the inner life is necessary, the alignment with the truth that can be found only in the soul of the person.

Much has to be recognized and actualized by us, so that we can achieve a true, deep spiritual success. For this reason, we need heroic sacrificial courage, in order to truly attain a firm alignment with the Highest.

Sacrificial courage means to fight your ego each day anew and, if we have spiritually fallen , to get up again and again.

What is a negative thought?

Every selfish, greedy thought. Envy, pride, denigration of our neighbor, jealousy, revenge, discord and stubbornness are contrary, negative thoughts. Base inclinations, too, such as alcoholism, compulsive eating, gluttony, smoking, resentment, humiliating others, vanity, arrogance and all compulsiveness, including compulsive sexuality, have their roots in self-centered, negative thoughts and sensations.

What is compulsiveness?

To be driven by a delusion is an aspect of compulsiveness. Or wanting to have the same things as the other, the greed for money and goods. Curiosity, wanting to know everything the other person says, is also compulsive. Fanaticism, too, can be considered an aspect of compulsiveness, depending on the intensity of this tendency. The delusion of wanting to discard all base humanness from one day to the next is fanaticism and can thus be compulsive. Excessive sexuality is compulsive, as is also being clouded by thoughts about a woman or a man, wanting to possess a woman or a man or wanting to achieve something with them. Everything excessive is compulsive.

And so, to extricate ourselves from our human aspects, we need order in our life. This is why we will now note down in our journal:

> *We put order in our life, in our thinking, in all our efforts and striving. By so doing, we attain the nobility of our soul. The result is a harmoniously balanced body rhythm that approaches the rhythm of the cosmic life more and more.*

By journeying into the kingdom of the inner being – that is, by working on himself, a hectic and nervous person becomes more still, his movements more harmonious and his senses finer.

We want to become selfless, so that our self-pity can fall away and we become aware of strength. This means that whatever we do, we do it with God and totally.

So, the first task was to pay attention to our body rhythm and to harmonize ourselves. We should avoid hectic movements. Fast, disharmonious walking leads to outer and inner disharmony as well.

This does not mean that we should put aside a dynamic life, the dynamism of our body. It means that we should strive for an inner, balanced dynamism, a spiritual dynamism, a noble, rhythmic movement of soul and body, and not a hectic, disharmonious state of being turned without.

And so, we practice the right discipline, to attain the harmony of soul and body.

Uncontrolled eating, fast chewing and hasty drinking also lead to disharmony. Through this, the body rhythm changes immediately. As soon as we fall back into disharmony, we also take up our old habits, which we thought we had overcome. Hot and very cold drinks also have a disturbing effect on the rhythm of the body. Very hot and very cold drinks cause a revolution in the nervous system. The nerves become tense. They suffer a shock. This disturbance affects the entire organism. This means that we fall back into hectic activity and inner agitation. Our movements, yes, our whole body rhythm, changes to the negative, to the disharmonious.

What I am now giving here is a repetition, only summarized, in order to bring the entire teaching material to mind again.

As soon as we become restless and agitated, it is often no longer possible to keep our thoughts under control. Our thoughts then race uncontrolled through our brain again. Through this, our soul and body move into low zones of vibration, into spheres in which completely dif-

ferent energies of sensation and thought vibrate. These can then become effective in us. And so, if we find ourselves on a low level of vibration, we will also attract the thought-complexes vibrating there and they will become effective in us. Thus, we will be influenced by the thought-waves that vibrate there.

We have to watch ourselves; we have to monitor our thoughts and counter the contrary, negative thoughts with positive ones, so that our vibration does not drop, which would result in a tensing of our nerves and body.

A hectic body, a tense nervous system is often no longer able to fend off the negative, contrary forces, which can take hold of our entire organism, depending on how far we have moved into these low zones of vibration.

And so, if we do not catch ourselves in time, by countering our negative thoughts with positive, constructive and life-affirming thoughts, we will be prisoners of our own powers of thought. Also, by constantly thinking about something, or by brooding about it, we intensify the negative forces in our soul and in our body. In this way, they will also influence us.

And so, an essential task for us is to pay attention to our thoughts and to our body rhythm. The prerequisite for this is a spiritual discipline and the will to put our thoughts in order and to counter the contrary, negative thoughts with positive, constructive and affirming, goal-oriented thoughts.

So that we achieve the constant alignment with the Highest, we have to heed many things: the monitoring and control of our thoughts, of what we say, of our body rhythm and the mastery of our five senses as well.

The five senses, the senses of hearing, of sight, smell, taste and touch, also need to be refined. The five human senses form the antennas to without. If our senses are coarse and unrefined, if they seek only in the temporal, then we are world-oriented, not God-oriented. For this reason, we have to refine our senses, so that, over the course of the ennoblement of our soul and of our body, we can grasp the Spirit in all things.

As soon as our senses become refined, we turn all our efforts, our striving and thinking, to within, to the Spirit in our soul. When we have established a connection to the origin of life, we will receive pure inspiration. For us, this often means working on ourselves, for several years or even decades, in order to attain the pure inspiration. When we have established the connection to our inner being, we will see things and events from within, as they are, and not as they seem to be.

So, the outer senses have to refine and turn within to the senses of the soul, so that the senses of the soul and the senses of the body attain <u>one</u> alignment, namely, with the divine life in the soul, with the core of being. If we have made contact with our infinitely eternal being, we will also see the positive in the world, in our neighbor *and in everything that lives, and we will live in a positive way. If we are attuned positively, we are merciful, kind, understanding, tolerant, forbearing and loving.*

We will record the following in our mystical journal:

The more we refine our five senses, the nobler our cast of mind and the purer our life. And so, the nobler our thinking and striving are, the more we are aligned with the Highest, with God, the life.

The second task is: Train your sight! Each day we should strive to align our sense of sight with the inner life, to thus attune it to the inner senses, the senses of the soul. We heard that the organ of sight is a very important sensory organ, for it affects all other senses. And so, we strive to conscientiously carry out this task given to us by the Spirit. I may repeat it again:

Until now, we have let our eyes roam, observing the world, with its stimulations and occurrences, as it offers itself to us. On the path to God, this has to change. On the path to God, we will examine ourselves more and more.

At first, we observe ourselves so that we may recognize ourselves as we are. We watch how we think about things and events and to what stimulations our eyes are exposed. We then we record the "for" and "against" in our mystical journal.

I repeat: On the right side of the mystical journal, we enter all that is positive, everything we believe we have dealt with, all that is good and noble. On the left side, we enter all the sensations, thoughts and stirrings that we could not yet overcome, that move us again and again, that burden us over and over again and draw our senses to without over and over again, into the world of the senses.

So, the right side of our mystical journal shows the light-filled sides of our life, all that we were able overcome for the most part. We should be glad of this and thank God for His guidance and help. But we should also thank God, our Father, for the shadowed sides that are recorded on the left side of our mystical journal and are not yet overcome. Through Christ, our Redeemer, God shows us what we may still overcome with the Spirit of Christ.

Out of love for God, we will then deal with our human characteristics and inclinations, the shadowed sides of our life. The person who goes to battle against his base ego consciously has Christ at his side, as support and help. Only with heroic sacrificial courage and the inner joy of victory will the student master himself.

Dear brother, dear sister, take your journal to hand and record the following sentences, which you should bring to mind again and again:

The love for God is essential, because the love for the Eternal enables us to overcome many things. The greater the love for God is, the more quickly we will surmount our human characteristics and inclinations.

The simple exercises given from the Spirit of God bring about a deep inner life. God is not complicated; God is simple. It is the simple that is so ingenious. This is why we have these simple exercises.

I may repeat the exercise for the organ of sight:
We look at a coniferous tree or a flower or a bush, whatever we like at the moment; however, it should be a plant. First, we look at it with our outer eyes. We look only at the external. We record into our mystical journal the thoughts and sensations that rise in us while doing this.

Then we look at the plant from within; this means that we try to take in its impression as a whole. We look at the plant. Then we close our eyes and let it reverberate in us. Again, we record in our mystical journal the thoughts and feelings which we perceive while doing this.

We can do this exercise several times, two or three times a day. Whenever we feel our senses being very strongly drawn to without again, or when our body rhythm changes, that is, when we become hectic, then we should do this inner contemplation again as soon as possible.

Dear brother, dear sister, may I also remind you of the soul prayer.
You have heard of the well that has to be cleaned out first to reach the pure source. So that we find our way to

the source and our soul prays lawfully, we first have to clear away everything that hinders the flow of the wellspring.

Let me also remind you of the greeting of peace. Dear brother, dear sister, do not become fanatic about this either, but greet your fellow man in the same way as he approaches you. However, greet the brothers and sisters who are on the Inner Path to God with the greeting of peace, with "Peace be with you."

The path of love is the path from the person to the God-person, from the base nature to the divine. God is absolute. We, His children, should become absolute once again. The most wonderful victory is to have vanquished oneself.

Where there is no love for God, there is also no path to God. Where there is only humanness, human existence, human willing, thinking and striving, there, the love of the Father cannot consciously enter. This is why we want to fulfill the tasks from the Spirit of God joyfully and thankfully, out of the love for God, our Father, and for our Redeemer, Jesus, the Christ.

May peace be with us all!
The brothers and sisters in Universal Life are linked with you in brotherly, sisterly love.
Have courage, dear brothers and sisters! Constancy in going to battle against our ego brings success. We

have all struggled and continue to struggle to draw nearer to the divine in us.

*Full of understanding and linked in divine love
from person to person,
from soul to soul,
from place to place,
into infinity,
I remain your sister,*

Gabriele

4. Lessons on Sight and Hearing, and Overcoming the Past

Everything is a revelation of God – God is the love – Recognizing correspondences – Exercises for training the eyes to foster the awareness of unity: contemplating minerals and stones; contemplating animals; contemplating nature – From training the senses to schooling the heart – The origin of thought – Memories and correspondences – Vagabond thoughts and ever-recurring thoughts – Letting the past rest – Forgiving and asking for forgiveness – A lesson on hearing: The effect of disharmonious and harmonious sounds on the body rhythm – Wisdom – Encouragement by Brother Emanuel – Summary: A good foundation; a step-by-step refinement instead of castigation; consciousness, subconscious, soul –
From the human to the spiritual; repetition of the tasks

Our sister, Gabriele, spoke to us from the divine Wisdom:

Greetings in God, dear sister, dear brother!
The peace of the Lord is with you.
The following teachings, lessons and tasks from the Spirit were given to us on the 11th of November 1984, by our spiritual teacher, Brother Emanuel, the cherub of divine Wisdom, through the inner word of the prophetess of the Lord.

It is the will of God that the Inner Path be revealed to all people, so that many may find salvation within themselves.

On Oct. 11, 1984, Brother Emanuel greeted the students on the level of Order with the following words:

Greetings from the heavenly spheres!
Greetings from the life, which is the life of us all!
Draw hope and confidence!
Become strong in faith and trust!

Brother Emanuel continued:

At every moment, God, the almighty power,
calls you through countless mouths.
God calls you in the innermost depths of your soul.
Every cell of your body is a revelation of God.
God calls you through minerals, plants and animals.
God calls you through the stars.
Everything is filled by His revelation!

Gabriele said:

Dear sister, dear brother, those of us who have taken a small step on the path within could experience that the person who walks inward to this great all-encompassing consciousness, God, truly feels that he is a child of the universal Spirit, a cosmic child. Although we human beings still feel the heaviness of the earth because the material garment is of this earth, we – who strive toward the Spirit – nevertheless have an inkling of the lightness of the inner being, the dynamism of the all-encompassing Spirit, the source of eternal love.

The path to within is the path of love for God, our eternal Father. Without love, there is no path to God, for God is love!

Dear brother, dear sister, for some of you it is still difficult to do the soul prayer and to carry out the tasks given by the Spirit.

We know that every beginning is difficult. As long as the brain cells are burdened with worldly matters and events, with important and unimportant thoughts, with envy and animosity, and our senses are still turned without, we will be distracted again and again from our spiritual exercises. In addition, our senses are constantly exposed to overstimulations, so that we do not find our way to inner stillness and to deep peace right away, from which the selfless life, the true I Am, the impersonal Being, can gradually emerge.

Dear brother, dear sister, we should not let ourselves be discouraged by our failures, nor by the opinions and conceptions of our neighbor. Become strong in faith and trust and become more aware each day that we are all cosmic children – not children of this world!

As long as we keep identifying ourselves with our person over and over again, and flirt with our human weaknesses and inclinations, we will feel the heaviness of the earth, which lies like lead over our good will and our good resolutions.

Only our love for God lets us become conquerors of the humanness in us.

Many people always ask us: What is love?

Love is the creative power that brings forth the pure life, the spiritual forms, and that gives life to the temporal forms, the material. Love is a band that links all that is pure.

We again begin to develop the love that sees everything as perfect. It is our spiritual heritage, which we accept again. The acceptance of this spiritual heritage, which is the creative, all-encompassing love, God, takes place step by step:

- *When we immediately forgive an upset person who wrongly accuses us, this is an act of love.*
- *When we pray from our heart and entrust ourselves in prayer to God and remain in this trust, this is an act of love.*
- *When we selflessly help our neighbor without expecting anything, neither gratitude nor a friendly smile, this is an act of love.*
- *When we do not condemn our neighbor who, knowingly or unknowingly, acts or speaks in a hurtful or degrading way, this is an act of love.*

Through these and similar demonstrations of love, we come into our heritage again. We grow into ever-greater spiritual tasks, which we fulfill out of love for God, without expecting thanks or anything in return.

In this way, we become conscious sons and daughters of God again, who gradually find their way out of the law of cause and effect, out of the wheel of reincarnation, and place themselves in the Absolute Law. They are themselves a revelation again, because they are divine again.

As long as we do not work on ourselves with the willingness to make sacrifices and do not counter our contrary, unlawful thoughts with positive ones, with thoughts of understanding, trust and love, if we let ourselves go, and let the past flare up over and over again in our thoughts, we cannot follow the path of love. We remain people among people who move in the flood of human thoughts.

And so, if we are always preoccupied with one and the same things, with our past or with present problems or with one and the same inclinations, it will become difficult for us to walk the Inner Path. If we are not yet willing to make sacrifices, it is too soon for the Inner Path.

Brother Emanuel said the following to us:

Dear students, fight the inclinations, the human sensations and base stirrings with the might of divine love – but do not castigate yourselves!

He continued:

On the path to the inner life, I teach you to train your senses, your heart and your soul. The human senses have to be refined more and more, so that the soul can purify itself, and the inner nobility, the nobility of the soul, can break through. Without the refinement of the human senses, the alignment with the spiritual, with the divine, cannot be accomplished, for the senses of a person are like antenna. If they are turned outward, they perceive external impressions, human thoughts, forces from energy fields and much more.

If the senses of a person are refined, they link with the senses of the soul and form the antenna, which are then aligned with the core of being of the soul, with the divine.

The Redeemer-spark in a person burns brightly only if he surrenders the burden of his base ego to Christ to be transformed – through the ennoblement of his senses, through a pure way of feeling, thinking, speaking and wanting.

Our sister, Gabriele:

And so, dear brother, dear sister, we have to go to battle against our base ego, so that the inner life, our true being, can make its breakthrough.

If the soul then awakens more and more in the Spirit of God, it strives toward inner discipline, toward selflessness, the impersonal life.

If our soul has awakened in the Spirit of God, if soul and person long for God, for His love, we will walk the path of love, the path to our inner being, joyfully.

Brother Emanuel said:

Many a one among you still has to awaken the soul, so that it may become aware of its divine origin and filiation, and strive for spiritual discipline in order to fulfill the will of the Lord. For this reason, the one student feels the path as a liberation, and the other thinks it is too difficult. You feel and think according to your consciousness and the maturity of your soul.

Brother Emanuel continued:

Dear students, we begin with the training of the senses.

In order to do justice to the inner senses, the senses of the soul, the external senses have to obey. The previous lesson began with the training of the eyes. I gave you simple exercises as, for instance, contemplating a coniferous tree or a plant.

The exercises have shown that the subconscious or the soul garments or even the consciousness aspects already developed by the person convey completely different impressions than an outer contemplation, the observation of something with the mind. The mind registers the external, matter. The subconscious or the soul garments or even the consciousness aspects already developed by the person can express something opposite to the mind.

The subconscious, the soul garments or the opened consciousness show how or who the person actually is.

Brother Emanuel continued:

Dear students, the correspondences, everything that soul and person have inflicted upon themselves in the course of their earthly sojourns, lie in the subconscious as well as in the soul garments.

The correspondences communicate with the consciousness. They also shape the person. How a person feels, thinks, speaks and acts, so is he.

The correspondences, the greater and smaller burdens of the soul and the subconscious, portray the person. The way a person speaks, what he thinks, his body structure, his body rhythm, his movements, all this is the portrayal of his correspondences. Since everything is based on radiation, the correspondences, too, radiate, and portray the character of the person.

Brother Emanuel taught the following:

Therefore, the student should pay attention to his correspondences, not to his mind. As long as the person does not coincide with the divine, he often speaks differently than he thinks, and thinks, in turn, differently than he feels.

To reach deep self-recognition, honesty with oneself is needed. The inner life of the person, the correspondences, have to surface. You have to become aware of them, so that you can truly recognize yourself.

The mind does not always tell the student, the pilgrim on the path within, what still lies in him and what characterizes his present nature. The mind deceives itself, by ignoring the correspondences, or by repressing them. The mind produces pictures thatth are human and thus oriented to this side of life. It produces pictures of how the person would like to be, and yet isn't.

Dear students, learn to recognize yourselves in your inner being. Learn to grasp your correspondences and to analyze them; then you will gradually get to the bottom of your problems and difficulties.

With the exercises I am giving you, namely to take into yourselves the nature kingdoms – that is, the essence of life in the forms of nature – I am trying to convey to you a slight idea of the unity-consciousness, of being related to all things.

Everything you observe, everything you see, is in you as essence!

Gabriele said to this:

Dear brother, dear sister, and so Brother Emanuel calls upon us to develop the forces of the inner being, so that the outer and inner senses gradually become refined, and we, soul and person, may find our way to the great stream, from which we all come.

> Brother Emanuel continued with the exercises
> for training the eyes:

You will now look at minerals and stones with your external senses, with your mind. In so doing, strive to be empty of thoughts, that is, endeavor not to think of anything, to empty yourself for the following exercise:

Now direct your sense of sight to a particular mineral or stone! If you have grasped the external picture, close your eyes and take the picture into your inner being. Try hard to stay free of thoughts! Wait for some moments until the picture becomes active in your inner being and conveys to you what the correspondences are signaling.

The person who carries out this exercise from the Spirit conscientiously will recognize very soon that the external senses reflect something totally different than the correspondences in the subconscious or in the soul garments, or even in the consciousness aspects already developed by the person.

After every exercise, record the following: Write down on the left side of your mystical journal what your external senses reflect to you. On the right side of your mystical journal, record what your inner being, the correspondences or the consciousness aspects already developed by you are conveying to you.

Our sister explained:

Dear brother, dear sister, in the course of the spiritual exercises, we will recognize that what is recorded on the right side does not necessarily have to be positive. The inner picture, the correspondences, can tell us something totally different than what the mind did. In a contemplation, the mind, that is, the person, can even praise God's omnipotence and affirm the nature kingdoms as divine, while the correspondences in us can reflect exactly the opposite!

And so, we can see that the mind – the person – often deceives itself. We often deceive ourselves, knowingly and unknowingly. But our inner being, that is to say, our correspondences, tell us far more. They show who we actually are.

In order to do these spiritual exercises successfully, we have to do justice to ourselves and strive to be empty of thoughts in the moments and minutes of the exercise: We do not think; we simply carry out the exercise.

I may repeat: You can do this exercise purposefully and recognize yourself in it, only if you are honest with yourself, if you do not drown out your rising correspondences with your mind, by giving excuses and self-justifications.

Dear brother, dear sister, you can do these exercises several times a day. Through them you will get to know yourself, who you actually are. You will become aware of what is human in you and what is spiritual and selfless in you. Through self-recognition you are given the opportunity to gradually reduce the humanness that you have recognized with the help of the Christ-Spirit in you.

Our spiritual teacher revealed:

So that you also get to know yourself in all the elemental spheres, and in time, learn that the essence of all forms of life is in you and that you are a part of infinity, you have to recognize yourself and experience the limitations, the human aspects, that still lie in you and that create the distance to the unity-consciousness and the All-consciousness.

The unity-consciousness is the unity with the nature kingdoms, with all people, beings and things. The All-consciousness is living from the Spirit of God.

Gabriele:

Brother Emanuel gave us another exercise, so that we recognize ourselves in all detail, including in the forces of the elemental spheres. Here, we look at animals, our favorite animals, as well as those animals that we still tend to reject.

This exercise is again like the first one: With our organ of sight, we again look at the outer picture, as Brother Emanuel has taught us. And so, the outer picture is registered by our brain, by our mind.

Then we close our eyes and take this picture within. This means, we let the outer impressions take effect in our inner being. Either our correspondences or impulses from the pure Being will rise in us. Both show us who we truly are. Again, we write into our mystical journal what these two pictures tell us: What the outer picture conveys to us goes on the left side, what our inner being tells us is recorded on the right side.

Dear brother, dear sister, you will now receive another task, so that you may come to know yourself ever more deeply and gain a very light sense of what unity-consciousness means:

Take in the nature kingdoms, the total impression of the outer forms of life that present themselves to you. This means that you do not look at the individual components of the nature kingdoms, such as a stone, a plant or an animal, but look at nature, at everything that lives in it, as a total impression.

Again, at first, the outer impression, the outer picture. Then, take in the total impression. Wait some moments, until the correspondences or the expressions of your consciousness rise up and convey to you what your inner being wants to tell you.

Write down the sensations and thoughts that you become aware of externally as well as internally. Record in your mystical journal again the outer impressions as well as the inner ones, the sensations and thoughts that come up in this process.

Brother Emanuel said to us:

With these exercises, I want to convey to you a small part of the unity-consciousness. And while doing them, you learn to recognize your base ego, which lies in the deeper layers, in your subconscious and in your soul garments. But you also find out the extent of your selfless love. The observation of the external and internal images brings out those sensations and thoughts, in which the student, the pilgrim on the path to God, can recognize himself.

Brother Emanuel said:

By training your senses, you will find your way to the schooling of the heart. Through this schooling, you will recognize very quickly that every unlawful sensation, every impure thought and every unlawful action turns against you.

The alert student who is aligned with God will then no longer wish evil onto his neighbor or condemn him. He will no longer entertain unlawful thoughts against his neighbor. His words will be noble and pure, because he knows that whatever goes out from him will fall back on him.

The conscious pilgrim on the path to God feels that God, the life, is in all Being. He knows that whatever he does to life he ultimately inflicts upon himself. The one who conquers himself and wants to progress on the path to God will strive to see the good in his neighbor and will also affirm it. It is the selfless power, the life of infinity. The pure and beautiful in your neighbor – it is the life, God – is in every human being, even in the one who is still marked by his ego and unconsciously betrays this through his words, gestures and actions. So do not judge, because through this, you will become your own judge.

The person who truly strives toward God will endeavor each day to meet his neighbor with his heart and not with his mind, because the mind disregards a person, seeing him as he thinks and speaks. The heart, however, is a gift for sensing, which lets one look deeper, which accepts the person, understands him and shows this understanding for him. This is the preliminary step toward selfless love.

Gabriele made us aware of the following:

Dear brother, dear sister, through self-recognition – to which Brother Emanuel wants to guide us – which, in many cases streams from the unconscious, from the correspondences that show us who we actually are, we will become more sympathetic and understanding of our neighbor, because we have come to realize that whatever annoys us about our neighbor still lies in us.

And so, we recognize that we are not flawless, but that we are encumbered by the same or similar faults as our neighbor. This makes us understanding. And from this understanding then grows the love for God, who sees us as perfect, who does not punish or chastise us, but teaches us the way back to the Father-house.

The person who gradually recognizes himself and struggles to become free of his "thinking in a personal way," of his base ego, will also gain a lot of understanding for his neighbor who, after all, is also struggling on the path to life. And no matter on which level our neighbor stands, regardless whether he is still with this world, he, too, will awaken the feelings of the heart, the true feelings for his fellow man and for all Being, through self-recognition and by struggling with himself to free himself from his base ego. And because of his self-experience and self-recognition, he then has the possibility to understand the Sermon on the Mount in the right way and to actualize it in his daily life.

Brother Emanuel gave us important advice
to take on our path. He said:

On the level of Order, you keep hearing: "Put your thoughts in order! Curb your speech! Master your senses!" Where do your thoughts come from?

Gabriele:

We will now go after our thoughts and come to realize that many thoughts flow from our sensations. We will take another step deeper and realize that many sensations rise from the burdens, from the correspondences of the soul and of the subconscious.

In the soul, too, there are memories of things and events that once burdened the soul and person. These were correspondences that are now settled and atoned for, and remain in the soul as memories. But external impressions of joy and pain can also leave their mark on the soul as memories. These were not burdens, but forceful or memorable events or occurrences.

And so, we should come to know the subtle differences between memories and correspondences:
When thoughts or images rise from memories, they help us to understand our neighbor or to recognize a situation correctly and to accept it as well. We do not get upset in the process, but stand above the momentary situation. We see it clearly and can handle it in the right way, so that it does not become a burden.

But if we react from our correspondences, then we are annoyed, perhaps even agitated or upset. We are not in control of the situation; instead we think or speak around the point, and our actions will be similar.

Brother Emanuel
gave us a further tip. He said:

Dear students, the more sensitive you become, by fulfilling the soul prayer and the tasks, the more easily you will be able to recognize a positive or a negative thought. When you have reached a certain degree of sensitivity, you will no longer be satisfied with analyzing your thoughts. In many cases you will pay more attention to your sensations and where they come from.

Gabriele:

Dear sister, dear brother, again and again we are asked if it is right for a person to be so preoccupied with himself.

If we are taking the first steps on the path within, it is good in order to recognize ourselves. We have to first walk from without to within. We have to soften the external, the humanness, the hard shell; this means we have to surrender our unlawfulness, and thus uncover what is within, the noble, the pure and beautiful, so that it can grow from within to without.

However, on the path within we should not look into every vagabond thought, to analyze where it comes from. In the course of our life on earth, countless thoughts fly toward us. They are vagabonds, thoughts that were sent out by people and are buzzing around in the atmosphere, looking for a victim where they can nestle in and multiply.

We do not follow up on such vagabond thoughts. We pay them no attention. We recognize these "flying objects" in that they briefly come to mind and then disappear. They do not upset us. The decisive point is that they do not annoy us. However, as soon as we often think about them and get upset about it, then the same or like like aspect is also in us. We will then analyze this insofar as these thoughts more strongly influence us and torment us.

Once we have successfully reached the third level on the Inner Path, we will be more closely linked with God in our daily life. What we have actualized then flows from us as fulfilled power, as a fulfilled life. Our senses will have turned within, and we have become finer, nobler and purer. Gradually, we become active in a selfless way. This means that we become people of the Spirit, who live more and more from within to without, thus becoming selfless servants of mankind. We will then no longer expect praise or recognition from our neighbor. We strive to live according to the law, to pray and work and, as we continue on our path, to let our activities become a prayer.

However, when we begin the Inner Path, we first have to work our way into our inner being and uncover it, so that it can then grow from within to without.

Brother Emanuel gave further tasks.
He said:

Watch the ever-recurring thoughts! When a thought complex or even a thought-complex keeps moving you again and again, then ask where they come from!

With this exercise, you will reach your sensations, which may be no more than stirrings. These ever-recurring sensations, thoughts and stirrings that burden you are the ones that should be looked into, that is, they should be analyzed: Where do they come from, and what are the causes of these bothersome influences?

These trouble-makers, the human sensations, thoughts and stirrings are often components that the person himself has created during this life. They appear especially when doing the spiritual exercises, because through the exercises human aspects come more strongly into movement. And so, through these exercises, desires, occurrences and conceptions will rise to the surface again. They are those things that have not been overcome, that lie in the subconscious and in the soul garments.

Therefore, give over the thoughts that simply come flying toward you! Let go of them and let them be transformed in Christ, in the Spirit of Redemption. However, you should analyze what continually moves, or even influences and oppresses you.

Many people keep bringing back, over and over again, what has long since become a part of the past. They move it in themselves for hours and days, thus intensifying the correspondence in their subconscious and in their soul garments.

I ask you to let the past rest as much as possible, so that it may gradually dry up.

When despite all efforts to let the past rest, events from this life come up, that is, if they keep coming up again and again, then you should look into these sensations and analyze them. The person who lives in his past cannot master what comes toward him day by day. He will not attain mastery over his life. He is subject to his human ego.

Gabriele said to us:

What can an analysis of the past that we bring into the present and move over and over again tell us? It may tell us that we have not yet forgiven our neighbor, who caused us difficulties in the past. Therefore, to overcome these aspects of our past, we should forgive or, if necessary, ask for forgiveness.

Guilt is very rarely one-sided. Most of the time, the one more strongly affected has also acted against his neighbor, at least in his thoughts. Thoughts are powers and negative thoughts also create a karmic debt, a guilt, as it were.

For instance, we were treated badly in the past by one of our fellow men. An outer picture, an external impulse, rouses our inner world of sensations. The im-

pressions from the past come to light again; the past flares up. If our life is not disciplined and self-controlled, we will dwell on the past for hours and days. By doing this, we enlarge our correspondences in our subconscious as well as in our soul garments.

Brother Emanuel asked us the following questions referring to our past:

The alert student will ask himself again and again: Why do I still think about past occurrences and events? What have I not overcome? What does the past want to tell me?

The one who has not overcome the past cannot master the present.

Gabriele:

And so, our sensations tell us more than our thoughts. They tell the serious pilgrim on the path within what he still lacks. Our correspondences and sensations tell us who we really are. Once we have recognized ourselves, we should act on it by fighting the unlawfulness, our humanness.

If we have wronged our neighbor, we should clear up the matter, ask for forgiveness and make amends for the harm we have done to him, so that we can progress on the path to life.

On the path within we will experience again and again that in all infinity nothing happens by chance. As long as we live with our consciousness in the four spheres of purification, we live in the causal law, in the law of cause and effect. If we acknowledge the causal law, this means we understand that, in the last analysis, every effect had its cause, either during this life or in former earthly lives.

In his revelation, Brother Emanuel admonished us:

Dear students, therefore, train your sensations! Learn to recognize yourselves more and more deeply! Through self-recognition and actualization, you will then – little by little – become free from everything that still preoccupies you today. You will also find your way ever more deeply into the eternal consciousness, God.

Through purposeful exercises, you will address ever deeper layers of your human ego to become free from it and enter into the all-encompassing I Am, into the Absolute Law.

Our sister said to us:

Brother Emanuel also admonished us not to become lukewarm and to repeat the exercises again and again, so that it gets easier and easier for us to live lawfully. We should also pay attention to our body rhythm as well as to our movements and gestures.

To recognize and test our own body rhythm, Brother Emanuel gave us more tasks. We now move on from training our sight to training our hearing:

The sense of hearing that is turned without perceives, consciously and unconsciously, loud and disharmonious sounds. We want to train our sense of hearing, so that the external noises no longer penetrate our inner being and we are able tune them out, thus enabling us to rest in our inner being more and more often and for longer periods of time.

We are working on ourselves from without to within, so that we are then able live from within to without.

And so, the task Brother Emanuel gave us
is as follows:

Dear brother, dear sister, you now consciously perceive the loud noises. They penetrate to your inner being. They affect your nervous system and stimulate the activity of your thoughts. These, in turn, affect your nervous system. Inner changes become evident externally in corresponding movements, gestures and ways of speaking. Thus, the external sounds, which vibrate in our inner being and influence our world of thoughts and our nervous system, are noticeable externally in our body rhythm.

Dear brother, dear sister, so test how the external, disharmonious sounds affect your inner being. Watch the stirrings and movements of your body. Record these experiences in your mystical journal. Write them down on the left side of your mystical book.

The other task is as follows: Now take harmonious sounds into your inner being – harmonious music or the harmonious song of certain kinds of birds, or the friendly and kind words of your fellow man – and let these harmonious sounds reverberate in you. The echo becomes evident again in your body. Now watch your body rhythm, your movements, your thoughts and words. Record on the right side of your mystical journal what you now experience and observe.

Our sister Gabriele explained to us:

Dear brother, dear sister, and so you yourself should experience the harmonies and disharmonies, what effect negative and positive thoughts have in your inner being and how they show themselves externally. Especially the body rhythm is very essential for recognizing and harmonizing ourselves.

From the revelation of Brother Emanuel:

Harmonious thoughts produce a harmonious body rhythm; the person is balanced and can think clearly and with concentration. However, disharmonious thoughts – thoughts of egocentricity, of selfishness, of hatred and envy, thoughts that only circle around one's own interests

– change not only the aura, the corona, which outlines the body and surrounds it as a halo of energy, but also become evident in a changed body rhythm.

And so, watch how your body rhythm changes when, for instance, you write faster, or vigorously scratch your arm or leg, or call out loud, or have a strong reaction because, for example, your child entered the room with muddy shoes, or when you wipe the floor hastily, or wash clothes with rapid movements ...

Haste is disharmony. Dynamism is rhythmic.

Hasty actions trigger awkward and jerky movements. Competitive sports or fast running change the body rhythm: The person becomes hectic.

Every hectic action that triggers a disharmonious body rhythm produces an increase in thought activity. If the thoughts are not recognized and dealt with accordingly – that is, if they are not given over and transformed into positive, understanding forces – then new causes can be created from this.

Hasty eating and drinking also change the body rhythm. Any hastiness gives indication of negative sensations or thoughts.

Gabriele:

If we do not pay attention to these phenomena in us, multiple causes can be the result. We create causes or intensify the correspondences that are active in us, which then show their effects.

When we bump into a table or the leg of a chair, we should pay attention to the reaction of our body and to the thoughts that follow: Whatever we think in this situation is still in us. But we should also ask ourselves what made us bump into the table or the chair. What were our thoughts, words or actions just before it happened?

All these exercises make us recognize ourselves: We experience who we truly are.

Brother Emanuel
explained the purpose of these exercises:

Dear students, everything that is unlawful in your inner being has to be brought into movement, so that the human aspects, the correspondences, in you may rise to the surface. In this way, you come to a deeper level of self-recognition, where you can find the root of your base ego.

A wonderful world opens up to the person who gradually conquers himself. He realizes that he is a cosmic child and feels free in the cosmic life, without being tied down and without fear. For he recognizes that when he lives in a positive way, only what is positive can come toward him. Whatever is still negative will flow out, but will not hinder him from continuing to strive more fervently for a life with God.

Whoever walks the Inner Path successfully will soon recognize that it is wonderful to live in the free Spirit, in the Spirit of Christ. It is wonderful for the person whose heart speaks and whose mind is but the instrument of his heart and, in subsequent development, the instrument of the purified soul.

Dear students, generally speaking, this is the path within to the absolute love. It is the path of love.

Brother Emanuel asked us a question which we should answer for ourselves:

How much has the love for God developed in your heart, the selfless love that unifies all things, that makes people free? The greater your love for God is, the purer are your sensations, thoughts and words.

For this, Brother Emanuel gave us a criterion by which we can examine how we feel, think and speak:

Which inclinations are still a part of you? Your love for God is accordingly so. The more nobly the person feels, thinks and speaks, the freer he is and the greater is his love.

And so, the inner being shapes the external. Your actions, your gestures, your outer appearance, change according to your inner development. Inner harmony expresses itself externally, in colors and forms, in your gestures and movements, in everything you do. The same is true for disharmony.

The person who walks the path seriously gradually takes off his mask, his individuality, and behaves as he is at the moment. And so, the person who walks the Inner Path successfully purifies his soul and his subconscious, so that his sensations and thoughts are his words.

Brother Emanuel explained to us:

A person's individuality is the personal, the human, the mask and what is hidden behind the mask. The one who takes off his mask has truly made great progress on the path of love.

That which is individual, the egocentric, is the human, the personal. A person who is impersonal is a divine being in the earthly garment, who feels and thinks divinely. But the individual works with what he has acquired externally, with his intellect. The divine, free person, the impersonal being, works with his opened consciousness. He lives and operates in this world according to his mentality and spiritual characteristics.

If the person sheds his individuality, he is not giving up anything. On the contrary, he receives much more, namely, divine wisdom!

An individual has only knowledge, but seldom wisdom. Spiritual people have knowledge and wisdom.

The mentality of your true nature should make its breakthrough, so that your inner being is reflected externally.

*Our sister Gabriele
addressed us again:*

In his name, I would like to pass on the encouragement Brother Emanuel gave in 1984 to the students of the intensive schooling:

Do not lose heart!
Be courageous!
The freedom in the Spirit of Christ is beckoning. Come and let the inner truth lead you and fulfill you!

Your brother from the light asks you to be courageous! Sacrifice your base ego! Truly, you will gain infinitely more.

Give up the baseness, so that you can live in the highest! Come and be ready: Join hands and call on the One who gives you the strength to draw nearer to Him, our Father.

Heaven bows to the earth and the powers of heaven become effective in those souls that love God more than this world.

Set out! Christ, your Redeemer, is so close to each one of you. He is the inner listener. Give your love to Him! Place before Him everything that hinders you from being selfless! Rejoice and be happy – your soul has heard the knocking of the Lord.

Dear students, my friends, my brothers and sisters, the blessing of the Lord goes with you. His love envelops you. Be of good cheer; the Lord does not forsake you. Be of good cheer; the love is so near to you!

Become selfless. Do not want anything of your own volition. Let the will of the Lord be done in and through you. Then you are also protected, enveloped in His great and mighty love.

Brother Emanuel took his leave with the words:

Greetings in God, my friends!

Gabriele continued speaking to us:

*Dear brother, dear sister, now follows a brief **summary** of the lessons and instructions from the Spirit that was given in a revelation, so that you can deepen your understanding of them once again.*

On the level of Order, the foundation is laid for the subsequent levels. The foundation should not be built on sand. This means that we should do the exercises diligently and joyfully, so that we can lay a solid foundation for the subsequent levels leading toward the divinity.

When we think of building a house, we know right away that the foundation must be laid first. We need to dig deep enough, so that the foundation has a firm hold. This means that the soil has to be removed; then the foundation is laid into the earth. Once the foundation is secured, one floor after another will be added.

It is similar with the Inner Path: So that we are able to start building up our inner life, we first have to dig from without to within. This means that we have to first stir up many things, everything negative in us, and remove all that is not spiritual, that burdens us. With specifically oriented exercises, we bring out a lot of unlawfulness from our inner being. We empty our vessel.

The foundation then is the ennoblement of our senses, the alignment with the divine, the peace and stillness in us. Only then has the foundation become secure. Subsequent floor can then be built more quickly, once the foundation is in good order. If it does not comply with the building codes, we have to keep working on the foundation so long until it stands on solid ground.

To master the level of Order is hard work! A good worker will lay a good foundation. A bad worker will lay a bad foundation. He will soon realize that he cannot build his house on this foundation. And so, the person who works on himself – out of love for God – will build a good foundation.

Someone who has little faith in God, or who has no love for God, will build a bad foundation. He will do the exercises that were given by the Spirit inadequately and thus, he will not build the foundation that he needs to be able to add on other floors. Let me repeat the words of Brother Emanuel, since they are very important for the Inner Path:

Without love, there is no path to God, for God is love!

In this revelation, Brother Emanuel gave the schooling of the heart and training of the senses. Those who still have no heart for God cannot go through with the training of the senses, since all the tasks will seem like a form of castigation to them and not like tasks through which they can overcome themselves, becoming free of intellectual thinking and attaining the inner wisdom, the divine wisdom. Every beginning is difficult, but the one who feels even a little love for God will in fact become a conqueror of his base nature.

As of now, the overstimulation of the senses is still there. The senses do not yet allow many a student to find his way into the stillness, into the deep peace from which the selfless life, the true I Am, the impersonal Being, wants to rise.

Brother Emanuel encourages us over and over again to become strong and to feel like cosmic children, not like children of this world. For instance, if we keep saying, "Oh well, I'm just a weak and simple human being," we are putting ourselves on the same level as the weakness of the human being. But if we say, "I am a cosmic child," imagining the cosmic powers, the life of the suns and planets, then our thinking and the direction of our life changes.

We lend strength to whatever we affirm, and this is what we hold on to. We do not want to hold on to our person. We want to recognize it courageously and overcome it joyfully.

We should fight our human sensations and inclinations, but not castigate ourselves! This means that we should gradually reduce our base inclinations, whatever they may be, even if it is still the overstimulation of our senses – through sensuality, through the pleasures of eating or of fighting. We should recognize ourselves in them.

This means that we should raise our thoughts and feelings to God, and then our human inclinations and stirrings will become refined. This, in turn, means that we do not repress them but refine them. Through this, all humanness will fall away from us bit by bit, until we can let go of all that is transitory from within. Therefore, we do not want to repress but to gradually overcome.

Castigation is repression. If we castigate ourselves, we are repressing something. We are pushing back whatever dominates us into the impure vessel.

Let me give you an example: When we drop a stone into a vessel filled with water, or press a dough-like mass into it, the water overflows and the objects in the water have an effect on us.

So if we repress what we should be overcoming, we push other tendencies out of the vessel. This means that whatever we have repressed shows itself in offshoots, in a craving to eat or to drink, in sensuality or irritation, in depression or aggression. As a result of repression, we also judge and condemn. We call our neighbor unloving, because we think we are better than he. All this can be the result of castigation.

For instance, if we have a strong craving for meat or sausage, we will not say, "Because I am on the path to God, I cannot eat meat or fish." We will link with God, knowing that we are cosmic children. We will then sit harmoniously at the table, aware that God is in all things. If we eat meat, sausage or fish in this awareness, the portions of meat or fish will become smaller because the Spirit-power, God, helps us to gradually change over to lawful foods.

The same is true for drinking. Here, too, we should not castigate ourselves. Hard liquor is not spiritual. However, it is not a matter of castigating ourselves, but of gradually reducing and slowly overcoming; it is a matter of gradually reducing the frequency of our intake of hard liquor and of reducing the contents of our glass. If we feel we are connected to the inner life while eating and drinking, if we are in harmony, then it is possible for us to reduce our food intake as well as change our drinking habits.

Therefore, it depends solely on us, on our thinking and wanting, on our attitude toward life, whether we will stagnate on the Inner Path or make determined progress.

The same holds true when we still cling very strongly to dogma. Brothers and sisters who are still strongly tied to the dogma of their church often say: We Christians do not have to do anything for our own salvation; Christ has taken away our sins.

Let us think about this logically: If Christ had taken away all sins or if He were to take them away from this point on without our having to do anything, we would now be flawless, and our whole thinking and striving would be selfless, that is pure. If we were pure, our earth, too, would be clean, and so would our food and everything that is for the benefit of mankind. But since this is not so, we have to ask ourselves whether this statement of church Christians is correct.

We know that Christ brought us redemption. He is our leader into the Father-house. We have to obey the leader, so that He can guide us. Obedience to Christ lies in the actualization of the eternal laws. For this reason, we have to work on ourselves, so that we actualize and fulfill the laws and can follow our leader, Christ, our Redeemer. If we actualize the laws, the Redeemer-light in us grows and we follow our Redeemer into the eternal land, into our eternal homeland.

Gabriele reminded us:

We began with training the eyes. The first exercise was to contemplate a coniferous tree or a plant. With this exercise, we realized that the mind reflects something quite different than, perhaps, the opened consciousness, or the subconscious and the soul garments. We realized that the mind registers the external aspects, as it is usual in this world. The subconscious or the soul garments or even the opened consciousness may occasionally reveal themselves as being opposite to the mind.

Our consciousness is our mind. Our consciousness is what is still in our memory, what we are familiar with, what we work with on a daily basis. The subconscious is the deeper layers of the brain, where what the consciousness has forgotten, those things we can no longer remember but have not yet overcome, are found. The shadows of our soul are found in the soul garments. The soul and soul garments show our correspondences, our burdens, that is, our karma, our soul-debt. In the soul, in the soul particles, are found the memories of what we have already overcome and no longer annoy us. And so, the memories, too, are reflected in the soul garments.

The correspondences that build up in the subconscious find their way into the soul if we do not recognize and surrender them in time. They become causes that we will have to bear as effects sooner or later.

The correspondences that develop in the subconscious can at first be memories of things past. But if we think about the past over and over again, if we get upset about it, thus adding new, unlawful thoughts to it, then these memories become burdens, correspondences, which bury themselves in the soul and are reflected in the soul garments and in the physical body. In this process, the spiritual atomic structure of the soul changes. The nuclei of the spiritual atoms turn more and more away from the core of being of the soul, from the divine, in order to register and absorb the worldliness, the will of the person.

The spiritual atoms in the particles of the soul are the spiritual senses. When we refine the external senses, the spiritual atomic structure of the soul – the corresponding spiritual atoms within the soul particles – also turns back again to the core of being and receives more energy from there. This means that our soul becomes lighter and our body brighter and purer. And so, it is a process of transformation from the human to the spiritual.

A process is always movement. Every movement brings with it agitation and unrest. This is also how it is on the level of Order, especially during the first lessons, when the obstinate person should listen to the Spirit and restrain himself. It is not our mind that tells us what kind of a person we are. Instead, it is the correspondences in our soul garments and in our subconscious that tell us what still characterizes us and what we should overcome in order to become free from our human ego.

In his revelation, Brother Emanuel gave us
a sentence that is important for us:

Whatever has not been overcome and cannot easily be dissolved has to gradually rise and reach your conscious mind, so that you can recognize yourselves.

Gabriele:

Our present nature lies in our correspondences, not in our mind. Though our mind may reflect many correspondences that are active in us, it can also deceive us.

However, if we recognize our wrongdoing in time and it is possible to release these negative forces that adhere to us from our inner being through specifically oriented exercises, then we do not have to expiate them or endure them. Let us recognize the chance, the divine grace, in this!

Another essential sentence
from Brother Emanuel:

Through these exercises for the refinement of the senses, I want to convey to you a tiny inkling of the unity consciousness, of your relatedness to all things, because <u>everything</u> that we see and that lives is in us.

Gabriele explained:

Dear brother, dear sister, think of the first exercise again, about the contemplation of minerals and stones. You can repeat this exercise from time to time, depending on your connection with the divine, until you have recognized and grasped what effect the power of nature has on your inner being.

Let me also remind you again of doing your soul prayer and of monitoring and controlling your thoughts and your body rhythm.

I would also like to remind you of the second exercise, on the contemplation of the animals – your favorite animals as well as those you still reject in your inner being and externally. During the contemplation, we experience that we like an animal, or reject another. This shows that we are in harmony with certain species of animals and have deliberately violated other forms of life – during this life or a previous one.

The same is true for plants, minerals and stones. We have to attain harmony with all forms of life. This is why we should become aware that the essence of all life is in us. If we deliberately violate life, we do violence to our soul and to our body. Whatever we send out comes back to us.

Another exercise I would like to remind you of is to take in the totality of nature.

Dear brother, dear sister, do not perceive the individual components of nature, but nature in its totality. This means to look at the external picture and let it work on you for some time. Then, close your eyes and take the picture within. Wait for a while and let the picture become effective in you. Then, write down the memories or correspondences that rise from your subconscious or your soul garments. Record on the left side of your mystical journal what the outer picture told you. Then record on the right side what the inner image conveyed to you.

The one who conscientiously does these exercises and tasks for training the organ of sight and is upright and honest with himself while doing them can now sense a tiny fraction of the unity-consciousness.

Once again a fundamental statement
from Brother Emanuel:

If a person still has little sensitivity and understanding, he has to reach the schooling of the heart and the development of his sensitivity by way of the training of the senses.

Gabriele:

If our senses have become finer, if our inner being, our heart, has opened for the cosmic life, then we will no longer wish evil on others, condemn them, or harbor negative sensations and thoughts. We will be positive toward the elemental forces of the minerals, toward the world of plants and of animals, recognizing that whatever we do to our second neighbor – the animals, plants and minerals – we also do to ourselves.

If we have gained understanding, if we recognize and acknowledge the life in all things, if we begin to love all Being, then love and selflessness will shape our inner being.

Our spiritual teacher revealed to us:

Through these exercises you will recognize that everything which, in the last analysis, is in you as purity and beauty, is also in your neighbor. Then you will meet your neighbor with your heart and no longer with your mind. You will see the pure in him and you will link with the pure, just as God sees only the pure in every person, in every soul.

Gabriele:

When we see and affirm only the pure, then the pure will also communicate with us, and we will gain love in return, and our inner being as well as our outer appearance will be marked by beauty.

On the other hand, when we see only the negative, the unlawful and impure, we will come into communication with these base forces – our nature becomes polluted, our senses coarse and our external appearance bestial.

Through the struggle with our faults and weaknesses, heart-feelings for our fellow man awaken in us.

Dear brother, dear sister, again a reminder:
On the level of Order you hear again and again: "Put your thoughts in order! Curb your speech! Master your senses!"
Where do thoughts come from?

Thoughts are born from sensations. Sensations can flow from the correspondences that are active in the subconscious and in the soul garments. But they can also flow from the pure, depending on how heavily our soul is burdened.

The more sensitive we become by doing the soul prayer and by fulfilling the tasks and exercises, the more we will give serious thought to our sensations. The alert pilgrim will strive daily to get to the bottom of his negative thoughts. He will go after those ever-recurring unlawful thoughts, that is, he will unravel them; he will pay attention to his sensations and find out where they come from. We now pay more attention to our sensations, which may be no more than mere stirrings in our disposition.

In the first stage of the Inner Path, the sensations and stirrings could come from this life, or from our consciousness and subconscious: Things we could not forgive, what moved and hurt us years ago, we keep bringing back to mind, stirring it up again. Impulses from outside or the exercises revealed to us help us recognize what is only covered up, but not forgiven and thus not overcome either.

We have to strive to gradually overcome the unlawful things that show themselves time and again, that keep reaching our consciousness through impressions and conversations. If we keep thinking about it, we intensify and solidify these complexes in us. Memories, too, can grow stronger and become correspondences, when we refresh them in our thoughts over and over again. Once they have reached a certain intensity, they go into the soul and become burdens.

Brother Emanuel asked us to let the past rest. But should things from the past, occurrences from this life, come up again, we should not take them into our world of thoughts right away and analyze them. We should strive to let our past rest. But if we cannot give over these stirrings and sensations, if they keep coming back when we send them away, then we will analyze them and ask ourselves what we want to gain from them.

We are our own sensations and thoughts.

If we analyze them precisely, that is, if we look behind our sensations and thoughts, then we recognize that we may not have forgiven our neighbor yet or do not even want to forgive him. So, we have to ask ourselves why we do not want to forgive. What do we want to gain from what happened in the past?

Our spiritual teacher, Brother Emanuel, revealed:

Forgive your neighbor who has wronged you. If you have wronged your neighbor, ask for forgiveness and make amends!

The one who recognizes that everything is based on cause and effect knows that, in the last analysis, whatever may have happened in the past also had a cause.

Therefore, train your sensations! Learn to recognize yourselves more and more deeply. Then you will gradually become free from all the things that still preoccupy you today. Then, dear students, you will find your way more and more deeply into your spiritual consciousness. Ever deeper layers will be addressed, so that you will finally be able to bring out, recognize and surrender the remnants of former burdens.

Gabriele:

Dear brother, dear sister, let me remind you of the training of the sense of hearing. The sense of hearing that is turned without consciously perceives loud, disharmonious sounds. We then take these dissonances into us, let them reverberate in us and let our sensations come. Then, we observe the reactions of our body.

Here, too, we recognize a difference: What effect do these disharmonious sounds have externally? And what effect do they have in our inner being?

Through this, we get to know our body, how it moves and which reactions it shows when we have unlawful feelings and thoughts, when things upset us. But we also get to know our body when we are still and harmonious. Our body rhythm also tells what we feel and think, that is, who we are.

Brother Emanuel announced to us:

Once the exercises and tasks have been done in depth, once they have become a part of your being, other tasks will follow. These will then be the movement of the consciousness and subconscious, reaching all the way to the soul garments.

Gabriele said:

With the following questions from Brother Emanuel, I will now conclude this lesson from his third revelation:

How great is your love for God? How far has your selfless love developed – the love for God that unites all things and makes the person free?

The greater your love for God, the purer are your sensations, thoughts and words. Here, too, the student has a criterion at hand with which he can examine himself: How do I feel, think and speak? Which inclinations are still a part of me? This shows how great or small your love for God is!

The more nobly the student feels, thinks and speaks, the freer he is.

Furthermore, the inner being shapes the outer. The actions, the gestures and the appearance change. The inner harmony is also expressed externally in the colors and forms that the person likes, in his gestures and movements, in everything he does.

*In closing, our sister Gabriele
spoke words of deep caring and encouragement:*

Dear brother, dear sister, the brothers and sisters of Universal Life wish you the inner growth and becoming, the ever growing love for God, our eternal Father.

We, too, are on the path to the Eternal and link with you, dear brother, dear sister, in the love of God. May His peace be with you and with us all!

Peace, dear brother, dear sister!

Gabriele

5. Self-Recognition by Training the Senses of Hearing, Smell and Taste

*Development of the senses
and order of thoughts – Fight before the victory – The divine
in all things – Man as sender and receiver*

*Task: Alternately turning the sense of hearing to within
and to without – Training the senses of smell and taste (inner
and outer days) – Conscious eating and uncontrolled food
intake – Fulfilling desires – Planning – Letting go and living
in the present – The "gliding" soul prayer – Love for neighbor
– The satan of the senses – Aging and inner youth – Inner
freedom and inner peace – Summary*

―

*Our sister greeted us
in the intensive school of the Inner Path:*

*Greetings in God, dear brother, dear sister,
may the peace of the Lord be with us!*

On March 17, 1985, our spiritual teacher and brother, Emanuel, gave a revelation for the level of Order to help us develop our senses and put our thoughts in order. And so, the teachings and lessons written here come from the divine world and are given by Brother Emanuel, the cherub of divine Wisdom.

Brother Emanuel
told us in his revelation:

Many a one among you still finds it difficult to walk the Inner Path diligently. This is quite natural. A person's physical body consists of cells that until now have obeyed only the outer senses. The army of cells has turned to outer influences, to the stimuli offered by this world. The cells still long for everything physical, not for the spiritual, lawful principles of life.

Gabriele:

We should endeavor to change our cells, from externalized striving to inwardness.

This means that a change has to take place in us, from an externalized life to inwardness. This is a fundamental change that takes hold of the whole person and also touches the soul accordingly.

And so, the cell structure – which, like everything, consists of atoms – should now become refined and turn toward the inner senses, the senses of the soul. This means for some of us to turn back and change our thinking completely.

In his revelation, Brother Emanuel
gave us the following explanation:

Even though competitive sports are not lawful, I want to use this as an example for a daily spiritual training:

Every competitive athlete has to train daily in order to give a good performance. Only perseverance brings success and victory.

Gabriele:

Dear brother, dear sister, we will not progress on the Inner Path without aligning with the goal, with God, and with our tasks, over and over again. We have to get up over and over again whenever we have succumbed to our negligence and laziness, in order to grow and mature spiritually. Those who have already made some steps on the Inner Path have had to realize that a person has to train daily to defeat his base ego, which always brings him difficulties and problems.

The base ego consists of different thought-forms, that is, thoughts that are emitted from a person, that form together and influence the sender over and over again.

We may no longer feed the thought-forms we have created, by thinking the same or similar way over and over. Instead, we should oppose these thought-forms with positive, divine forces of selflessness and peace, of good will toward our neighbor. We will then starve these thought-forms out. They will withdraw from us and transform into positive energy.

We know that our person, our ego, brings us only difficulties and problems. Despite this, we hold on to our ego.

We should frequently ask ourselves the following questions: Why do we hold on to our difficulties and problems? What do we want to accomplish with this? For example, if we repeatedly complain about the same disagreeable situation, it will not improve. Quite the contrary, we just intensify it. If we talk about one and the same situation over and over again, we have to ask ourselves what we are trying to accomplish with this.

And so, we want to keep disagreeable things, including difficulties and problems, because we want to gain something specific through this. Perhaps we cannot forgive one of our neighbors. Perhaps we accuse God because of our situation – even though we know that we ourselves are the originator of our fate. Perhaps we are trying to blackmail our neighbor into doing what we think is right.

Every one of us will have to recognize one day that before victory comes the fight with the base powers, with our base sensations, thoughts, words and actions, with our externalized senses that strive for good living, for an inconstant life. Our externalized senses keep trying to draw soul and person to without, to the external forces, into the world of sensual stimulations and pleasures.

Dear brother, dear sister, in the meantime you have learned to train your organ of sight. You have also had a glimpse of the unity-consciousness. Many a one among us has sensed and felt what it means to experience everything as a whole, the power that flows from without to within, making the soul peaceful yet activated, at the same time. The one among us who has sensed this unity-consciousness and feels it anew each day also feels the genuine fulfillment of his life. He recognizes and senses that God, the almighty power, is all-ruling.

The divine spark is in all life forms. The divine spark is consciousness; it is life. Thus, every form of life is consciousness – according to its development. When we affirm the divine in everything that is, we receive strength from without, from the nature kingdoms and the stars; for the divine, the consciousness, is in all things – and especially, in man himself. If the consciousness communicates with the divine consciousness that is in all life forms, including man, then the divine powers flow.

Whoever sends out the powers of selfless love will receive the powers of selfless love many times over.

Dear brother, dear sister, we, too, who are on the further levels, had to learn all these things and live through them until we realized that without actualization, there is no goal in sight.

Many a person thinks that if he had a lot of knowledge he would be wise. However, knowledge is not wisdom. Knowledge is the prerequisite for becoming wise. Only when we apply our spiritual knowledge on ourselves, by actualizing God's laws, do we become wise: We become completed consciousness again. We are still in different states of consciousness, because as long as we are tied to the causal law, we are in the so-called states of consciousness, according to our spiritual development.

On the Inner Path we learn that there is a constant flow of positive power. It streams to the one who opens himself for the positive powers. The divine power also streams to us by way of the nature kingdoms and the stars, as well as from those people whom we love selflessly. Through this, soul and person receive strengthening.

To be able to receive the powers of the nature kingdoms and of the stars, the precise alignment of soul and person is necessary.
Everything is consciousness. If we have not refined our senses and have not aligned our being with God, we can receive only very little of the divine power.
We human beings are senders and receivers. Let us think of our radio and television sets. If we have not tuned in to a station, we will not receive. We may hear the noises or frequencies of several stations, but we will not hear one station clearly, because we have not properly tuned in to the station.
The Spirit of our Father sends untiringly. Everything is permeated by this sender, the Spirit. If we are not aligned with this sender, God, through actualization, through an attunement to Him, then we cannot precisely receive from Him either. We may perhaps receive impulses from some transmission ranges that are not of

divine origin, but are thought-forms or forces from the atmospheric chronicle. If, because of an inconstant life, we receive several senders at the same time, we will burden and ruin our nervous system over the course of time.

An important sentence
from our spiritual teacher, Brother Emanuel:

Dear friends, the path to within is the path of love for God. Out of love for God, the student should gradually let go of his human aspects, so that he attain the divine.

Gabriele said to us:

Now we come to further tasks on the Inner Path, which are necessary to attain the refinement of the senses and the sensitivity of the soul and person.

We have already spoken about the sense of hearing, and that a person has to also school his sense of hearing, to make his inner senses so sensitive that the direct guidance by the Spirit of God in Christ, our Redeemer, can take place later on.

Since we live very much in the world with our senses, every single sensory organ has to be addressed individually.

Curiosity is a sign that our sense of hearing is oriented toward the outer world of appearances. The aspirations of a person who is turned toward the world are often to listen in on everything and find out everything he can. People of this world like to take notice of things and to follow them up. And so, curiosity is a sign that the sense of hearing is directed to without. However, on the path to the divine it should become refined.

Surely, everyone of us has experienced on himself that by constantly trying to hear everything, to register everything and absorb it, we become restless. Our nerves pull and tear and wear down our body. Yes, they do wear down our body, because curiosity is wasted energy.

Brother Emanuel gave us
an exercise to serve in self-recognition:

The following exercise should be done in alternation:
For two days, the student should strive to live within. To live within means that he should protect himself from negative influences: He strives not to take noises and sounds, that is, dissonances, into his inner being.

Gabriele:

This is done as follows: We may very well hear the noises and sounds around us, but we do not get annoyed about them.

By getting annoyed over the dissonances – no matter what they are or where they come from – we automatically take them into ourselves. They then affect our nervous system, making it tense and causing our spiritual and physical energy to be reduced.

Any tension can be traced back to disharmony, which has a disruptive effect on the organism. Every disharmony is based on the wrongdoing of a person, on an infringement of the eternal law.
Through our annoyance, we also activate a correspondence in our soul. This correspondence then comes into vibration and attracts exactly what annoyed and annoys us. This changes our body rhythm and we drop into a lower sphere of vibration, because dissonances take energy away from our body, thus causing the organism to slip into a correspondingly lower vibration. This means that it is then influenced by corresponding forces that linger in that particular sphere of vibration.

In his revelation,
our spiritual teacher, Brother Emanuel, said:

Disharmony expresses itself in uncontrolled thoughts and in many words. It also expresses itself in disharmonious, that is, hectic and abrupt, movements and uncontrolled actions. The person does things that are useless. Through this he wastes spiritual and physical energy, falling into the corresponding sphere of vibration that he chose himself through his wrong behavior.

Gabriele explained the exercises:

And so, we do our best to live inwardly for two days. We do our best not to take in the outer, negative sounds and tones; we do not let them enter us. We may very well hear them, but we just let them bounce off us. We live inwardly.

To become aware of this life within, we do our best to affirm the beautiful, noble and pure in nature and in all people, to see the good again and again. This brings about an inner readiness and a gradual growing into living in the Kingdom of God. During the inner days, we should keep to essential conversations and avoid all that is not essential. What our neighbor says to his neighbor is of no interest to us on the inner days. During this time, our sense of hearing is turned inward, in order to find rest and stillness there.

In order to open the door to the inner life, it helps to use consciousness aids such as:

I am the stillness.
I am the peace.
Everything in me is still.
I am peaceful.
I am harmonious.

These consciousness aids help us to overcome our rising curiosity, so that our inner being remains attuned to positive reception. When loud and shrill tones sound too intense for our ears, we should not reject them brusquely. Even in the loud and shrill sounds, we can affirm the positive, the power, which is quietly active in them, being encapsulated by the external, by the dissonances, but nevertheless present, for no sound is without divine power.

Through our steadfastness in affirming only the positive, harmonious sounds, the loud and shrill tones gradually become weaker in and around us, since we create a spiritual cocoon around us through our positive life, a spiritual energy field, which repels the greatest dissonances. In this way, we gradually find our way to inner peace.

Dear brother, dear sister, record on the right side of your mystical journal what you have sensed or thought during the two inner days – that is, the essential aspects of your sensations and thoughts.

Now come two outer days: On these two outer days, our sense of hearing turns outward. We take into our inner being the noises and sounds that the world offers us. By doing this, our curiosity awakens again. We pay attention to what the other person has to say again, to what the neighbor may be doing, what he is buying, etc. We do not overdo it, for example, by deliberately inducing the process. We simply let what the days bring us happen. On the left side of our mystical journal, we record the sensations and thoughts that come up on these outer days and perhaps admonish us.

These exercises can often be repeated, but not continuously, perhaps once every two weeks.

This alternation – living inwardly for two days and then again outwardly for two days – sets things into movement within us. Through these exercises, the consciousness and subconscious, as well as the burdens in the soul garments, are addressed in a lawful way. Gradually and lawfully, these exercises cause as much to rise in us as we are able to recognize and put aside. Thus, they serve our self-recognition.

Those who do these exercises without fanaticism will receive each day only so much to recognize as they can bear and actualize. Without self-recognition there is no remorse, and without remorse and surrendering one's faults and weaknesses – also called sins – to Christ, there is no liberation from guilt.

It must be stressed that these exercises, like every lawful exercise, have to be done without fanaticism. We should not force anything, but rather strive honestly and sincerely to give over to Christ what we have recognized. We should not suppress our faults and weaknesses either, but should instead give in to them less and less often, reducing them step by step. Then piece after piece gradually falls away from the complex of the human ego – and we become free from it.

At the end of every week or every month, depending on how intensively we walk the path, we should take stock of our progress in our journal: What have we overcome, what still needs to be done? We should be happy about what we have overcome and recognize that we are making progress on the Inner Path.

However, we should not let feelings of guilt about the shortcomings that are still there come up in us; instead, we may recognize ourselves again in them and overcome them with the help of God.

With the following words, Brother Emanuel
gave us an additional task:

The students on the path to the inner life also train their senses of smell and taste.

People who want to refine their senses will not consciously register the smells and fragrances that reach their organ of smell everywhere they go and are. To consciously register means to think and speak about the smells in detail.

*In the schooling,
Gabriele pointed out the following:*

Therefore, we should not stick our nose into everything, not even into a fragrant pot of meat.

Brother Emanuel
admonished us with the following words:

Thoughts and words are forces. They have their effect in and around the person who, for instance, thinks about the smells and talks about them at length and holds his nose over the source of smell.

When, for instance, a person talks about unpleasant and bad smells, he intensifies this vibration in himself, because smells and fragrances, too, are vibrations. By doing this, he attracts the smell-complex, which then influences him. These vibrations then have their effect upon the organism. They increasingly affect the senses of smell and taste and stimulate further cravings of the senses. The person will then be driven by his senses. His desires are what move him, craving this or that. They stimulate the person to acquire this or that or to eat a certain food.

Our sister said to us:

How often have we not experienced in ourselves that a mere smell stimulated us either to eat some sweets or to think a similar chain of thoughts, or to buy coffee, alcohol, cigarettes or the like? So, we end up being driven by our senses that are turned without.

Brother Emanuel revealed:

This state of being driven leads to disharmonies and tensions in the nervous system. This, in turn, leads to playing with thoughts or words, which draw the person into spheres of lower vibrations, because soul and body are losing energy.

On the other hand, natural fragrances, such as the scents of flowers, bushes and trees, stimulate a person. They stimulate the soul and produce in soul and body the harmony that flows from the pure forms of life to the person who is aligned accordingly.

Whoever ennobles his senses attains the nobility of his soul and finds the way to his spiritual consciousness, to the sonship or daughtership of God. In all that is pure, noble and beautiful lies the power of love, which is activated by selflessness and radiates through soul and person, shining over the entire organism.

As soon as the organ of smell perceives smells and fragrances, they are at the same time registered by the sense of taste. The organs of smell and taste transmit their perceptions to the brain cells, which immediately register these vibrations and influence all other sensory organs.

Gabriele added:

Dear brother, dear sister, now we will also train our senses of smell and taste. We do these exercises in the same way as the previous ones: Alternating two inner and two outer days, we find out again what shortcomings still remain in us.

On the first two days, we endeavor not to take the smells and fragrances into our inner being. We pay no attention to them. We do not stick our nose into everything that smells, not even into soup kettles or roasting pans. We will not think about smells and fragrances, nor talk about them. We have heard that with thoughts and conversations we only intensify what comes flying at us.

On the two inner days, we endeavor to <u>consciously</u> take in the fragrance of flowers, bushes and trees. We will not dismiss gentle and mild perfumes, but we want to consciously take in the natural fragrances.

We again record our impressions, sensations and thoughts on the right side of our mystical journal. We will also record what our palate signals to us on these two inner days. Thus, our journal tells us who we still are.

During these two inner days, we will take in our food in a disciplined and concentrated way. Through a disciplined and concentrated intake of food, our sense of taste is refined. Every bite that goes to our organ of taste should be chewed consciously and harmoniously.

We should take time for our meal. Every meal should be a holy act that expresses our thankfulness to God for the food He gives to His human children.

To eat in a disciplined and concentrated way also means that we fill our mouth with food only when it is empty, when the well-chewed food has passed on to the organ of digestion, the stomach. Once we have chewed our food well and swallowed it, we fill our fork or spoon again with a medium-sized bite.

Through this harmony while eating, we also ennoble our senses. The ennoblement of our five human senses then also has a positive effect on our soul. In this way, we help to ennoble our spirit body and the nobility of our true being gradually breaks through.

Another effect of eating harmoniously is that we gradually come into a higher vibration and base thoughts and compulsive desires do not fly at us or move us from within so often. We know that many things can dry up in us, without our having to live or even suffer through them. Correct and well-mannered eating habits contribute to inner harmony.

What happens when we are already busy with our spoon, fork or knife while we are still chewing on the last bite? As soon as the next bite is on our fork or spoon, but the last one hasn't been swallowed, our stomach urges us on and the chewing process is accelerated. The insufficiently chewed food that goes to the stomach may – in the long run – not only lead to complications like stomach troubles, but can also trigger various disharmonies, because the stomach and other organs have to work more intensely and thus use up too much physical energy.

The person who eats in an uncontrolled and hasty manner will also cause his organs of smell and taste to turn more and more to without and to crave more food and drink, as well as all kinds of culinary delights.

The same is true of the intake of liquids. The contents of a glass should not be emptied all at once, even less when it is ice cold. People on the path of ennoblement drink in sips.

Time and again we are privileged to realize that as soon as we refine our senses, our soul and our entire body structure are also refined. At the same time, our soul garments become lighter and we attain a continuous alignment with the incorruptible power, with God, the core of being of our soul.

And so, on the two inner days, we will become aware of what we are and will aspire to the inner nobility, by refining our senses.

So that we bring our consciousness, our subconscious and our soul garments into movement in our inner being, we will again go through two outer days. This means that the two inner days are again followed by two outer days. On the two outer days, we will let the senses of smell and taste have free rein again. What we heeded on the two inner days is disregarded on the two outer days.

The old habits reappear: While we are still chewing on one bite, we automatically, as usual, fill our spoon or fork for the next one. Another old habit is to drink with a full mouth. This, too, is permitted on the outer days, but it should not be forced; this means that we do not castigate ourselves. We do not force ourselves to do something we are not used to. Thus, for two days we will live just like we used to live before we had this spiritual knowledge and insight. All that we were able to register on the two outer days, the essential thoughts and feelings, we again record in our mystical journal, this time on the left side.

Dear brother, dear sister, it is up to you whether you do these exercises or not! No one forces you to do anything on the Inner Path. You can do these exercises every two weeks, once a month or not at all. Or you can start them once you have recognized that they will contribute to the refinement of your soul and body, once you have realized that through this exercise and through actualization, your conscience becomes freer and tells you more and more what your shortcomings still are, in and on you.

In his revelation,
Brother Emanuel reminded us
of the law of freedom:

It would be of little help and contribute little toward your spiritual edification, if as your teacher I were just simply to say: "You must do this and you should let go of that." Every person has free will, also on the Inner Path.

Gabriele:

It is necessary for all of us to hear this repeated. We have to experience for ourselves what it means to live inwardly, purifying and ennobling ourselves, or to remain on the outer level, to bustling about in the world and missing the goal. Through self-recognition, that is, by experiencing ourselves on our own body, we become willing to affirm and walk the spiritual path more and more, so that we may attain liberation from our base nature.

To be free means to have ever fewer worldly demands on ourselves and ever fewer desires and claims on our neighbor. As long as we have an attitude of expectation, as long as we expect something of our neighbor, that he do this or that, we remain tied to his opinions and conceptions. A person's heart is not yet free for the Inner Path who still makes substantial worldly claims for himself, who constantly circles his thoughts around his own interests, by wanting to possess this or acquire that – which pressures him and clouds his mind.

Our spiritual teacher, Brother Emanuel, revealed:

Every one of you still has smaller or greater desires. Whoever walks the path to God should examine himself to see what is necessary. Smaller or greater desires that do not push you or cloud your mind, but are simply there for the enjoyment of external things, should be fulfilled wherever possible and according to one's possibilities.

People on the Inner Path will not allow vagabond thoughts to distract them nor let unfulfilled, unimportant desires put pressure on them. They plan and weigh wheth er something is necessary or not. In thoughts, they then give their plan into the hands of the eternal God, including those wishful thoughts that cannot be fulfilled, given their present way of life.

A person who preoccupies himself a lot with his own smaller and greater desires causes his senses to turn without again and dissonances to enter his soul and body. A person who entrusts himself to God and builds on Him will receive what he needs – and beyond that.

Gabriele said the following about this:

God, the almighty power, can guide everything in such a way that it is good for us and serves the good of the soul. God helps us through ourselves and through second and third persons.

Our sister then added a few words about planning:

Dear brother, dear sister, we human beings are in the habit of questioning everything we do or plan. We seldom place what we have planned under the will of God. We make a plan and we then try to carry out this plan on our own. While we do this, we are constantly weighing our plan, whether it will be successful or whether, for this or that reason, it will not be possible to carry out what our desires are urging us to do.

By affirming it on the one hand and at the same time denying it on the other, by aimlessly working on the success of our plan, we are not only questioning our own work, but often contribute to its failure.

We should let God guide us more and entrust ourselves to Him. This does not mean, however, we should be idle.

Oh no! We should simply be the glove on the hand of the Lord. We should make plans and put our plan as well as our actions in the will of God. This means that we no longer doubt that the plan will succeed. We no longer weigh it. We work and act for our plan. We do not let ourselves be influenced by urging and gnawing thoughts. We contribute to the success of the plan, with self-possession and knowing that if it is God's will, He will guide all things and fate in such a way as it is good. In this trust, we work, act and live. This is trust, concentration and alignment.

And if it is still good for us, our desire will be fulfilled and our plan will succeed. If it is not good for us, it will fail. We should accept both, the success as well as the possible failure.

If, however, we start weighing the outcome beforehand, while questioning our project, we hinder God in

His works. By being torn here and there, by weighing the pros and cons, by affirming and doubting, we may even achieve the success of a plan that is, however, not good for us. We are then confronted with this success, because through our doubts and human reactions we turned away from the workings of God and opened the gates wide for base forces, which then worked for us, fulfilling our desire or even achieving a semblance of success of the plan. Through our human stirrings, we have in this case worked either with energies of thought from the atmosphere or with extra-terrestrial energies, with unlawful energies, or even made contact with souls that fulfilled our plan true to our desires. In view of this apparent success, we then continue pursuing our plan, work accordingly and finally, after months, years or in later incarnations – since we continue in a new life on earth exactly where we left off – we fail, because in the final analysis the plan was not good for the development of our soul.

Our doubt, mistrust, anxieties and worries bind us to our desires and conceptions, to people and things. The person who wants to find inner freedom must first become free from all outer ties and things.
As long as we want something of our own will, this is a so-called attitude of expectation. Every attitude of expectation leads the senses without, which then bind themselves to people and things. As long as a person wants something, he binds himself to people and things.

If he places his will under the will of the Lord, if he allows himself to be guided – instead of letting his human thoughts and desires pressure him – he will become free.

The more free a person becomes, the less demands he makes on the world and on his neighbor. He becomes selfless and gives; and the more selfless he becomes, the more he will receive.

The same is true for our planning. A person who plans in the right way, without desiring anything, without thinking and worrying about success or failure, is guided from above, by God. A person who knows that he is just a steward of his possessions and thinks of the well-being of his neighbor, that is, who no longer clings to his goods and belongings, but simply administers them, will receive more than he needs.

Whoever directs all his aspirations and ambitions to within, to <u>the One</u> who is the fullness, will also receive for himself from the divine fullness, in this world and in the other world.

The purer our souls become, the more we will receive externally, because the fullness comes toward the person who has opened the fullness in his heart and in his soul. This can happen in this life or in one of the following lives.

Happy is the one who recognizes this in time. He will then engage himself in the right measure, not for his own interest, but for the good of all, for the well-being of those who strive for the inner fullness.

In his revelation
Brother Emanuel spoke:

The one who sees himself just as a steward of his property, which God has entrusted to him for the common good, can let go of his ambitions to be, to have and to possess.

To let go means he is no longer urged by his wanting to be, to have and to possess. To let go brings peace, inner stillness, joy and harmony. People who can let go no longer live in the past. Nor do they think fearfully about the future anymore. They consciously live in the present.

God lives in the person who consciously lives in the now, and God is active through him. The Eternal lends wings to his soul, leading soul and person to undreamed heights.

And so, whoever schools his senses in the right way, who refines them and ennobles his thoughts, will find inner freedom and reach true greatness. What is it that takes place in the soul of a person who refines his senses?

First of all, his soul and soul-garments become more light-filled, because the eternal power transforms many things which the person then no longer has to bear, having refined his nature, his sensations and his thoughts.

Secondly, the spiritual atoms gradually align with the incorruptible core of being of the soul, with the central light, the primordial power. Increased energies then flow from there into soul and body.

These increased forces coming from the core of being have a positive effect on soul and body. The increased life force brings about health, happiness and contentment. As a result of this increased energy flowing from the core of being, God, the spiritual consciousness of the soul also expands. Soul and person become more still and more receptive for the eternal power.

Brother Emanuel explained to us again:

On the level of Order, by refining his senses and monitoring and controlling his thoughts, the student strives to work his way from without to within.
Once the student has refined his senses, put order in his thoughts and curbed his speech, from then on, he will live more and more from within to without. This means that the student has mastered his past for the most part and lives in the present. He will then shape his future with God.

Gabriele:

Brother Emanuel admonished us to fulfill the tasks and lessons given from the Spirit of our Father consciously and conscientiously, so that we may become free of our base nature and our spirit-consciousness may become still and expand at the same time. Only with a still and expanded consciousness can we aspire to higher levels, where higher ideals and values are a basic condition. The still and expanded consciousness of a person who lives in actualization is what anchors him in the divine.

A person who has taken some steps on the Inner Path, who through selfless thoughts, inner stillness and concentration feels selflessness in himself can – if he wants to – do the soul prayer from now on as follows:

Brother Emanuel gave us
the following suggestions:

At the usual time and in the same place, where you find peace and quiet to a certain extent, you fulfill the joyful task, the soul prayer.

The student assumes the usual upright sitting posture, and closes the five gateways of the senses. The first gate is the eyes. The second gate is the sense of hearing, which he turns within.

The third and fourth gates, the organs of smell and taste, are inactive. The fifth gate, the sense of touch, is also closed.

His hands rest on his lap.

The student consciously prays into his inner being with words similar to the following:

"Eternal Father,
my aspiration and striving
is to please You and to draw closer to You.
My senses are silent.
I want to penetrate to the eternal consciousness,
to You, eternal One,
You, who are, from eternity to eternity."

Gabriele:

Dear brother, dear sister, you can say this prayer to the Eternal according to your own sensations. Brother Emanuel gave us the above wording only as an example. Our words of prayer are accompanied by our thoughts and sensations. Only when our sensations and thoughts are with our words of prayer, do we pray with concentration. We direct the prayer within.

With sensations of love and thankfulness to God, we then glide to the consciousness center of Order, which is anchored near the coccyx region. The prayer energies now stream down to the consciousness center of Order. Once there, we address our soul in thoughts or with words. Here, too, it is important that each person pray according to his momentary feelings. Brother Emanuel's words should be taken as an example. They are as follows:

"Lord, You are omnipresent.
My soul and all my body cells jubilate to You.

My soul, attune yourself to God,
the omnipotent power,
and pray fervently to the One who has called you:
Eternal Spirit, You are in me,
and I want to be consciously in You!"

After this short prayer of thanksgiving, calmly and strong of faith, we linger in the consciousness center of Order. We remain still. No thought enters us. We let the soul pray. Selfless prayer sensations start to come. They rise up and take shape as thoughts and words.

After the prayer of the soul, we accompany the prayer streams with our sensations to the core of being of the soul. Once there, we give thanks in our own words.

Instead of speaking the prayer words aloud, we can also pray in our thoughts. In this case, we glide down to the consciousness of Order in our thoughts and our sensations are completely aligned with our thoughts.

Brother Emanuel
gave us another lesson. He said:

My friends, dear students, it is written: "Whatever you do to the least of My brothers, that you do to Me." What do these words mean?

They mean that whatever you do to your neighbor in your sensations, thoughts, words and actions will turn against you. Because of your human, egotistical sensations, thoughts, words and actions, you increase the shadows in your soul.

But the more selfless your sensations, thoughts, words and actions are, the greater the light in you will become. If you think positively about your neighbor, if you see the good in all things, the divine in the person, if you affirm the positive power in everything, then the soul will become more still and the person more conscious. This means he will think, speak and act more consciously. Through this, the Eternal can, in many cases imperceptibly, effect the purification of soul and body in the soul and person. Through this purification, the Christ-power in the soul becomes stronger. The soul becomes lighter and the body purer and brighter.

But if a person speaks about or treats his neighbor negatively, the negative will turn against him, as well. His body will darken, his soul will become shadowed, because the light of Christ in soul and body reduces. In this way, the person falls into light-poor zones of vibration. The shadows, which have developed in body and soul as a consequence of wrong behavior, then lead to further causes, on which the person again builds new causes.

The more shadowed soul and body are, the less spirit power flows into both bodies, the soul body and the physical body. The result is fatigue, listlessness and lack of peace. As a result, the senses increasingly turn without, to the world of the stimulation of the senses. There, in the outer world, the restless person looks for strength and life energy. Very often food is then the only way out. Because of his inner impoverishment, the person desires more and more food. He also turns to alcohol and tobacco and craves culinary delights.

Satan once said to Jesus: "Behold, I will give you all the treasures of this world, if you fall on your knees and worship me." And still today, using manifold ways and means, he gives the treasures of this world to those who turn away from the eternal light, turning toward the world, toward external things, and throwing themselves into the hustle and bustle of the world and worshiping the satan of the senses.

The return to the world or a life with the world are signs of spiritual impoverishment. When he does this, the person becomes ever more lethargic and negligent. Lethargic, negligent people who are oriented solely to the world grow old much faster than spiritual people, people of the deed. This inner impoverishment manifests itself externally, despite the care of the body, despite health cures and bath therapies.

Gabriele encouraged us with the following words:

Dear brother, dear sister, who among us does not want to stay young? Despite the natural aging process, we keep striving toward youth. It is an inner inkling, an inkling of the soul that knows about its eternal youth.

Brother Emanuel said the following to us:

My friends, people of the Spirit do not age – they fade.

What does it mean, to fade? Recognize: A leaf that withers on a tree can be very beautiful. Who would ever speak of an "old" leaf? Only the one who is old himself!

He continued:

My friends, I wish you the spiritual initiative. I wish with all of my heart that you walk the path within joyfully. Because in spiritual joy is the dynamism of soul and body as well as inner youth.

The more spiritual power flows through soul and person, the more dynamic and youthful he is. Even at an advanced age, the posture of such a person will be upright, because his cast of mind is upright. The nature of a thoroughly spiritualized person is radiant, loving and filled with inner strength and dynamism. Even though his external body may fade in accordance with the natural laws, the traces of inner, everlasting youth are maintained in him.

Gabriele:

Dear brother, dear sister, the brothers and sisters on the Inner Path smiled as Brother Emanuel said:

My brothers and sisters, it is worth your while to walk this Inner Path, if for no other reason than not to age.

As we can see, the spiritual world, too, can make us smile at ourselves.

Brother Emanuel encouraged us
to strive toward inner freedom:

Let go, my friends, let go of the past! Do not worry about the future. The Spirit of our Lord is so near you. He, the Almighty, wants to become effective in you and to give you the fullness.

The more you honor this eternal Spirit, by fulfilling the laws, the richer you will become in your inner being. Your life will be quiet and joyful. People who entrust themselves to God will truly receive what they need – and beyond that. Those who are imbued by the spirit of love are happy, glad and thankful. The spontaneity of their inner being is also the spontaneity of their external life.

Our sister Gabriele said:

Dear brother, dear sister, with his words which are flowing from his heart, Brother Emanuel, our spiritual teacher, wants to totally come toward us. He spoke and speaks to us:

My beloved brothers and sisters, with all my heart, with all my spiritual sensations, I want to encourage you to follow this Inner Path.

Oh recognize in my words the strength and love of your teacher that are flowing toward you! I want to lead you out of the tribulations of your daily life, to the eternal peace in you – to Christ.

Verily, my friends, the one who has found his way to inner peace can give peace in turn. He is the bringer of peace, whom this world needs. A Kingdom of Peace can be built and led only by peaceful people. What good are all the external things, if a person is not filled with peace, joy and dynamism?

Christ, your Redeemer, speaks of the Kingdom of Peace. You are all called to found and build this Kingdom of Peace with Him. May each one of you recognize the task, this great, mighty task, in himself. Each must first awaken to peace in himself before he can bring peace to the world. Therefore, each one should feel responsible, so that the Kingdom of Peace can emerge. But it can become only if you become!

Dear friends, if you walk this path of inner love and inner peace joyfully, thankfully and fulfilled, and if you are peaceful, a blissful joy will lend you wings and you can then bring this to all those who thirst for justice. Only the one is just toward his neighbor who is just toward himself in his thoughts, words and actions, and whose sensations and thoughts are the same as his words. The person who is just toward himself has found the inner peace and is the co-builder of the Kingdom of God.

My friends, words say but little. Grasp the <u>meaning</u> of my words and recognize that the Inner Path is necessary so that the Kingdom of Peace can emerge. And so, the person who walks the Inner Path successfully is truly a co-builder of the Kingdom of God on earth. After this life, he will return victorious to the eternal homeland. He will be no stranger there.

My friends, my beloved brothers and sisters, actualize and fulfill the tasks joyfully! Rejoice each time anew, when the moment has come to do the soul prayer again. The soul prayer renews your alignment over and over again, and at the same time ennobles you a bit more.

My friends, my beloved brothers and sisters, may the blessing of the Almighty support and encourage you more each day to do what is necessary to find inner peace, so that you can soon draw from the eternal consciousness, for the Spirit shall consciously rule over matter.

Greetings in God, my friends!

Brother Emanuel
gave a brief summary:

Victory is always preceded by the fight against the base forces, against the base sensations, thoughts, words and actions, against the outer senses, which seek to live a good life, an inconstant life. The senses of a person will keep on trying to draw soul and person to without, to stimulate him with temptations, until the person takes command of his base ego and lets higher powers become effective in him.

The following statement is essential for every student on the Inner Path:
The person who affirms the divine in all that lives and actualizes the divine laws also absorbs the positive powers of nature and of the stars. The one who emits forces of love will receive forces of love many times over.

Another important statement:
The path within is a path of love. Out of his love for God, the pilgrim to the kingdom of the inner being should gradually let go of his humanness and affirm the spiritual, applying it lawfully in his daily life.

Gabriele:

Dear brother, dear sister, I want to remind you once more of the training of the sense of hearing, of the tasks which are important for us, to gradually remove our ego from our inner being, all those things that we are not yet aware of but which nevertheless cause us difficulties and prevent us from finding unity with all people and with God.

Dear brothers and sisters, I would like to remind you again of the consciousness aids that are a help to us on our path when rising curiosity, desires and longings want to overpower us. Despite these exercises, we will con-

tinue to do our work – wherever we have been placed – in an orderly fashion and in inner harmony, aligned with the power toward which we strive.

I may repeat: In all loud dissonances we should also see the divine, because the divine is in all things, even in loud tones, being merely encapsulated by what we have emitted in sensations, thoughts, words and actions. No sound could be produced, if the harmonious power were not present in it as well. The divine power is partly covered up by the human being, or it is transformed into a loud, shrill tone, just as we transform many things that later may prove to be our undoing. By steadfastly affirming only the positive, harmonious sounds, we create a spiritual cocoon around us that gradually softens the shrill sounds around us, so that they do not have their full effect.

Dear sister, dear brother, please do not forget to record your sensations and thoughts on the inner as well as the outer days. Later, you will realize how valuable these notes are for you, because they will show you that you have already taken some steps on the Inner Path.

We should refine ourselves. The coarse structure of the human being is to be ennobled and spiritualized. The refinement of the senses of smell and taste is also a part of this. Please do not forget that everything that has turned without is also coarse, that is, impetuous. By heeding the divine laws – by putting our thoughts in order, by curbing our speech and mastering our senses –

higher vibrations will get a hold of us and flow through us and then increasingly reveal a soul in the process of ennoblement.

I now want to give you a sentence to think about:

The person who finds joy in the beauty and fragrance of the flowers, bushes and trees, and who senses the divine love in these life forms, increases the harmony in his soul and body.

Dear brother, dear sister, also when eating, remember that you want to ennoble your senses of smell and taste. Sit upright while you are eating and try not to eat hastily. Chew well, swallow what you have chewed and only then take another bite onto the spoon or fork and bring it to your mouth. Do this consciously and you will realize how harmony and peace can be with you also during your meals. When you eat in this manner, it becomes a conscious, meditative exercise of thankfulness. The same is true for drinking liquids. We should not gulp the contents of the glass down all at once, but drink in sips. The drink should not be too hot, but also not too cold.

Brother Emanuel revealed:

If the senses of a person become refined, the entire structure of his physical body becomes refined as well. At the same time, the soul garments become lighter and the soul nobler. As a result of the external refinement, the inner being is also refined. Through the refinement of the external senses, the atomic structure of the soul changes at the same time. The spiritual atoms gradually turn toward the core of being, toward the heart of the soul.

Gabriele repeated important statements:

Dear sister, dear brother, we have to gather experiences, so that we are ready and willing to follow the spiritual path more and more. If we have experienced what takes place in us on the inner days as well as on the outer ones, we will move on to the next exercise joyfully and will repeat the current exercise over and over again.

We have to become free from our human ego. The base ego ties itself to this or that desire. The base ego binds itself to people and wants to bind people to itself.

To bind also means to have an attitude of expectation. I expect my neighbor to do this or that; I expect him to behave in this or that way. As long as we remain in this attitude of expectation, as long as we expect something from our neighbor – that he do this or that – we are not free. We are tied to our ego and, with our ego, to people, things, desires and conceptions.

Additional important sentences for us:

If our aspirations and ambitions are directed inward, to the One who is the fullness, if we want to please God and not people, then we will also receive what we need; for God gives Himself to us to the extent that we open ourselves to Him.

The purer our soul becomes, the more we will receive externally, because the fullness comes to the one who has opened the fullness in his heart and in his soul.

Dear sister, dear brother, clear up your past. Whoever lives in God no longer lives in the past, just as he no longer thinks anxiously about the future. He lives in the present! God lives in and through the person who lives in the now, in the present. His soul is carried as by the wings of an eagle.

Selfless love brings inner freedom. The person who has found inner freedom has true greatness. If we have largely mastered our past and strive to live in the present, then God, the almighty Spirit, will shape the future with us.

Dear sister, dear brother, may I remind you once again of the soul prayer: Please pray using <u>your own</u> words. Pray as you feel in your sensations! Let it pray from your inner being or in your inner being. Each one of us has to experience for himself what is better for him at the moment: the spoken prayer, a prayer with words, or the silent prayer, a prayer in thoughts.

We let the following statement of the Lord resound in us: "Whatever you do to the least of my brothers, that you do to Me." *This statement means that whatever we do against our neighbor in our sensations, thoughts, words and actions will turn against us.*

If we think positively about our neighbor, if we see the good, the divine, in him, our soul will become more still. Unnoticeably, the Eternal purifies soul and person. Through this, the Christ force in our soul increases. The soul becomes lighter and the body brighter.

But if we speak negatively about our neighbor, the negative, too, will turn against us. The body darkens, the soul becomes shadowed, because the light of Christ in our soul is reduced. The person falls into zones of vibration that are poorer in light. The shadows, which have appeared in soul and body because of our wrong behavior, then create further causes. Upon these we can, in turn, build new causes.

The more shadows there are in soul and body, the less spiritual power flows to both bodies, the soul body and the physical body. The result is fatigue, listlessness and lack of peace. This causes the senses to turn more and more without, into the world of the stimulation of the senses. There, in the external world, the restless person then seeks strength and vitality. Large quantities of food, stimulants and drugs are then often the only way out. We start turning to alcohol and tobacco and crave more and more culinary delights. These are signs of spiritual impoverishment. In this way, the person becomes more and more lethargic and negligent. If such a person is given a task he is unwilling to do, he immediately falls into resignation, because he was pulled out of his lethargic state.

Every feeling of resignation leads, in turn, to unlawful sensations and thoughts. These may then create further causes and lead to a relapse into other human stirrings and inclinations of the past. Such people age very quickly. They may already look unsightly while still in the middle years of their life. They tend to be corpulent and weighed down by the load of their thoughts and deeds. The body is bent forward, the trunk unsightly.

*Our sister Gabriele
repeated a statement of Brother Emanuel's:*

*People of the spirit do not age, they merely fade!
Recognize this huge difference: We do not age; we fade. This means that the inner youth remains, that through the strength of the Spirit the dynamism remains, even into old age. So it is only our body that fades, since it is subject to the laws of nature; the spiritualized soul and the spiritualized person do not age.*

Concerning this,
Brother Emanuel said the following:

A leaf that withers on a tree can be very beautiful. Who would ever speak of an old leaf? Only the one who is old himself!

These statements from Brother Emanuel, repeated by our sister in their essence, are also important for us:

The more the spirit power flows through soul and person, the more dynamic the person is. Even in the advanced years of his life on earth, a spiritual person will walk upright, because his cast of mind is upright. The nature of a thoroughly spiritualized person is radiant, loving and filled with inner strength and dynamism.

And so, my brothers and sisters, it is worth it to walk the Inner Path, if for no other reason than not to age.

The composure of a spirit being can tell us such things in straightforward language.

Thus, the path within brings freedom and peace in us. For this reason, we should walk it joyfully, so that we may attain the nobility of our soul. People who are imbued by the spirit of love become happy, joyful and thankful. The spontaneity of their inner being is also the spontaneity of the external.

Dear brother, dear sister, we want to endeavor to fulfill the will of our heavenly Father, so that His Spirit can consciously rule over matter.

We wish you His strength and His love, so that you make steady progress on the Inner Path!

May His love link us and may His peace flow through us!

May His power lead us ever closer to Him, who is our life, God!

*The peace of the Almighty is with us.
Linked in His Spirit, we greet you,
your brothers and sisters in Universal Life.*

Greetings in God, dear brother, dear sister!

Gabriele

6. Training of the Sense of Touch

The uncontrolled sense of touch – Seven-times-seven aspects of consciousness – The person as the plaything of his outer senses – Everything is vibration – The person as the target of different forces

Exercise: conscious touching; alternating outer and inner days – An upright cast of mind and an upright physical posture – Excessive gesticulating and a harmonious posture

Exercise: an "excursion" into the cosmos – Communication with the beautiful, positive forces in everything – Questions for women and men (the second mask, the beard and long hair, clothing) – "Sense of humor," clothing and celebrations of love in the spiritual world – Summary

———

At the beginning of the new lesson, received from the Spirit of God, our sister Gabriele spoke to us:

Greetings in God, dear brother, dear sister! May the peace of the Lord inspire us all, so that we may understand and actualize the following teachings, exercises and questions revealed to us on April 13, 1985 by Brother Emanuel, our spiritual teacher.

We heard that we should refine our five senses, so that we grow closer to our origin. Our subject of instruction on the spiritual level of Order is the training of our sensations, thoughts, words and of our five senses. Our teacher, Brother Emanuel, reminds us over and over again to walk the path within joyfully and aligned with the highest love, with God.

Tasks and exercises were already given for the refinement of four of our senses. Each day we must align our senses anew and remind ourselves to think positively again and again, until we have grown to such an extent that we basically do everything from within, until it is possible for us to draw from our opened consciousness and be guided from within. This is then deliberate, conscious living; it is purposeful and constructive living.

The fifth sense, which we now address, is the sense of touch.

Dear brother, dear sister, if we look at the five senses from the point of view of the Spirit, we recognize that, in many cases, our hand wants to touch what our physical eye perceives. Our eye wants to see the smells and fragrances that are absorbed by the nose. The sense of touch reacts simultaneously. For instance, a person reaches for an object with a fragrant content and brings it to his nose. Attracted by the kitchen smells, he goes to the stove, lifts the lid off the pot filled with fragrant, cooking food and "sticks his nose in it," to fully absorb the smell. We could continue with such or similar cases, of which there are many examples.

If we are in town, in a department store, and we see a pretty fabric, our sense of touch immediately compels us to touch it. When we see furniture in different colors and forms, and we have the opportunity to look at them more closely, then we want to touch them as well, to examine them and to think about them. When we walk through the garden or take a walk through the fields and forests and when we see beautiful flowers, then it may again be our senses of sight, smell or touch that compel us. We want to take a closer look at the flowers; we want to smell and touch them.

The five senses imperceptibly control our mind as well as our world of thoughts and sensations. Our desires and conceptions, too, are prompted by the five senses. They cause us to pursue the desires of our senses and, to intensify with our thoughts whatever is in us as desires, conceptions and human or spiritual qualities. This is how we are controlled by our senses. This is why we have to refine them.

So, the person who has not put his senses in order constantly tries to touch everything he sees and registers. Our sense of hearing, for instance, calls us to the window when outside one neighbor is talking to another. Hastily and without control, we run to the window or balcony door to open it and perhaps lean over the balcony and listen in on what the two neighbors are talking about.

All these stirrings and inclinations are human and the more we pursue them, the more they lead us into the world of the stimulation of our senses. This increases our curiosity, our compulsions, our addiction to stimulants and many other things. Our uncontrolled senses lead us to without more and more, causing our worldly desires to grow more and more. This wishful thinking stimulates our thoughts about wanting to possess, to be and to have. This gives rise to envy, animosity and resentment, if we want the same or like thing as someone else.

Everything is based on vibration. We know that every one of us lives on a different level of consciousness, according to the way he thinks and lives. As long as we human beings are still individuals, clouded by our base ego, we are seldom of one mind with our neighbor.

Every spiritual level of consciousness – there are seven altogether – contains in itself all other levels. Thus, every basic level of consciousness, seen as a whole, has seven aspects, seven spectral lights. These stream from the primordial power as <u>one</u> power, as <u>one</u> ray. They are refracted in the prism suns, which orbit around the Primordial Central Sun. Thus, the level of Order, too, has altogether seven aspects of consciousness. It contains in itself all other spiritual levels of consciousness, namely, Will, Wisdom, Earnestness, Patience, Love and Mercy.

The spiritual heritage that God has given us consists of the seven-times-seven forces. It is the Absolute Law, God; it is the fullness of infinity; it is the consciousness, God; it is our life. We have to rediscover this life – our life – by acknowledging the laws and by actualizing them.

We will then find our way back into the fullness, into the Father-house, into the law that we are and that created us.

Via lawful thinking, rightful acting and thus, spiritual living – by submitting to the will of God – we find our way back to the origin of the source, from where we once went forth. And so, we are called to open in us the seven basic forces of life, to become free, in order to be one with God.

To open all seven basic forces, we have to begin with the first one, with Order. This is why we make every effort to put our thoughts in order, to curb our speech and to master our senses, so that we gain a stable foundation upon which we can build the subsequent spiritual levels. This is why the sentence that Brother Emanuel gave us in 1985 is of great importance for our life. It is applicable to all spiritual levels, whether we have reached them already or still have to develop them. He said:

As a person feels, thinks and lives, so is he. This is his nature. This is his realm of knowledge, his developed consciousness.

Dear brother, dear sister, please write this sentence down in your mystical journal to remember it. It is essential for the Inner Path and can be rediscovered on every level. I repeat Brother Emanuel's statement in its essence:

As a person feels, thinks and lives, so is he. This is his nature. This is his realm of knowledge and the level of his developed consciousness.

Dear brother, dear sister, as long as our five senses are still turned toward the material world, if possible, we want to see everything, to listen in on everything, to smell agreeable odors, to taste good food and drink and to touch everything we can possibly reach. This does not mean that we should give up and let go of everything that is beautiful and pleasant. It means that we should not crave it, but rather feel grateful for these things, and not allow ourselves to become enslaved by them. Any exaggeration, like, for example, fanaticism or letting-yourself-go, does not lead to inner stillness.

We know that our five senses are like five antennas. The five senses, the antennas, are constantly intent on transmitting to us, the human receiver, everything that we want, that we can reach and grasp. If our five senses are not purified and ennobled, if instead we are still driven by our senses, we cannot live from within to without. Our five senses, which are directed to without, take hold of us again each day and turn us into a plaything of our own desires, passions and compulsions.

If we look at ourselves and watch our five senses, we have to realize that we are as our senses are. And so, we are the product of our five senses.

For this reason, we can say that in the last analysis, we are our five senses. If we do not refine them, if we do not learn to control them, they will make of us an object without will that is driven once here, once there, just as our uncontrolled senses want it. This game the senses play with the person can lead to further soul burdens, if he does not get them under control, because they will increasingly influence his world of sensations and thoughts.

Therefore, the person who gives his senses free rein will absorb many vibrations that are the same or similar to his correspondences. Based on his five senses, which control and give him little room to maneuver, he goes from one field of vibration to the other. And so, he is a plaything of his senses. We human beings will continue to be the plaything of our own senses, until we have brought them under control. Once we have ennobled our senses and our thoughts, we will live more and more from within to without, because the goal of the Inner Path is to journey to the kingdom of the inner being from without to within and then to sense, think and act from there.

As soon as our senses, our sensations and thoughts are ennobled and obedient to the inner life, we will touch and take into our hand only what is necessary; and we will do so consciously, that is, closely linked with God, feeling and thinking from our inner being.

So, once we submit our thinking, feeling and willing to the Eternal, we are also protected from the many unlawful vibrations, including viruses and harmful bacteria, which can penetrate us when we are oriented to the world.

Brother Emanuel revealed the following:

Unknowing people touch everything they can lay their hands on, everything they are interested in. So people touch furniture, fabric, clothing and many other objects. Everywhere, they leave behind their traces, that is, their vibrations. On every chair, for instance, there are countless vibrations from all those people who have used this chair over the years. Vibrations of all sorts are on all material objects. And so, a person who is not in command of his sense of touch, because he has not refined his five senses and brought them under his control for the most part, and therefore still lives in and with the world of the senses – thus being oriented to this side of life and not God-conscious – accepts and absorbs all vibrations that are vibrating on his plane of consciousness. He becomes infected with them and identifies himself with them.

Gabriele:

The vibrations that we absorb with our sense of touch, with our hands, flow first into our aura. Our aura is the mirror of our soul, of our consciousness and subconscious.

Correspondences, memories and developing correspondences are found in our consciousness and our subconscious, as well as in our soul garments and soul particles. All of these are thought-complexes, that is, energy fields, which we created through our wrong way of thinking and acting. Some are strong, others less so. They are our emotional and physical burdens that vibrate more or less strongly, depending on the intensity of the individual thought-complex.

Our spiritual teacher, Brother Emanuel, explained about this:

A thought-complex, also called an energy field, can intensify and expand when the same thought is entertained over and over again. One thought after another joins in the correspondence that already lies in the soul, or in the developing correspondence, thus forming an ever-greater unlawful energy field, which has a magnetic effect on the aura, attracting equally or like vibrating thoughts from the realm of thoughts. Even expiated burdens that still exist merely as memories can be stimulated through a renewed wrongdoing and become correspondences again.

Gabriele:

This is why we have to daily make every effort to get our human aspects under control. This does not mean that we should castigate ourselves! We should gradually, that is, successively, conquer ourselves; this means, we should bit by bit reduce what is human in us and no longer do it.

The correspondences that have a magnetic effect on our aura are energy fields that attract everything on this particular wavelength. Through our uncontrolled sense of touch, we absorb such thought vibrations that cling to the object we touched and that are like our correspondences.

These forces, the thoughts, the desires and longings of others that are similar to our correspondences, first flow into our aura. If the same or like things are then always thought or spoken by us, then these outside forces touch our correspondences, either in the consciousness or the subconscious or the soul garments, depending on which correspondences are active in us and which vibrations we absorb.

If we persist in focusing on a certain matter and want to push our will through – for example, if we are envious, filled with hatred and the like – we may awaken memories in our soul, by letting the unlawful flow in, which then comes toward us as correspondences. Memories of the soul are effects of causes that we have already expiated, that is, settled, either in this life or in one of our former lives. So, when we pay no attention to our thinking, feeling and wanting and give free rein to our senses, we will either intensify the correspondences that are active in us from outside, and even expand on them, or we will reawaken memories – that is, matters that have already been settled – and have them become correspondences again.

We have to realize that a thought-complex, a correspondence, is the target of different forces, which we absorb from the outside without realizing it.

If we are oriented to the world – that is, if our senses, our antennas, are directed to without, to the world of the stimulation of our senses – then we are a target for various energy fields present in the atmosphere as well as in the spheres of purification. Souls, too, which vibrate similarly to our thought-complexes, to our correspondences, can then influence us. And viruses and harmful bacteria can thus gain access to our body.

If, for example, we radiate thoughts of fear about a certain illness, or certain pathogens, then our fear will be the magnet that attracts what we fear. And so, the one who lives in an uncontrolled way, that is, without monitoring and controlling his sensations, thoughts, words, actions and senses, is constantly at the mercy of unlawful human and astral forces as well as viruses and harmful bacteria.

The task of the soul in the earthly garment is to ennoble itself, so that it draw nearer to its goal, the divin-

ity. When we live more closely linked with God and communicate with the positive forces in us, in our neighbor, in nature and in the stars and planets, we will also absorb only positive forces, including the positive forces adhering to material objects, such as furniture, chairs, fabrics, clothes, etc. The positive forces serve us; they foster the spiritual in us and prepare us for higher things. Positive forces contribute to our spiritual and physical strengthening and to the stimulation of our nervous system. In many cases, they keep away viruses and harmful bacteria and lend wings to our positive sensing, thinking and feeling.

Our sister gave us another task:

And so, dear brother, dear sister, when we touch something, whether at work, at home or underway, we should do it consciously, from within, in communication with the Eternal.
Our spiritual schooling on the Inner Path thus has the effect that we work more with our stabilized and expanded consciousness, in order to grow nearer to our inner goal, to love, peace and harmony. In this way, the nobility of our soul comes to the fore, since our soul is purifying itself and receiving ever more light and strength, the beauty from the realms of eternal love.

Dear sister, dear brother, we all know that we human beings often cannot understand or do not want to under-

stand what we are taught by the spiritual world. Because of this, in many cases we have to endure the effects of our wrongdoing and experience them on our own body. Nevertheless, we want to strive to grow spiritually through self-experience and actualization, so that we need not suffer through all the causes created by us.

If we ourselves experience the effect of the lessons and tasks revealed by Brother Emanuel in and around us, we will be willing to fulfill the given tasks joyfully and to put them into practice. By doing so, we can spare ourselves much suffering, because recognizing and eliminating in time our self-made causes brings peace.

And so, with these exercises, we want to train our sense of touch and experience in ourselves how necessary it is to refine our senses.

And so, we will again live two days from within to without, and then again two days externally, that is, without monitoring and controlling our senses. This alternation, two days from within to without and then two days without monitoring and controlling our humanness, has the effect that we become aware of many things that lie in our subconscious, perhaps from the past, which we can then transform with the strength of Christ.

During the first two days, the inner days, we will touch everything that is necessary from within, from our consciousness. And so, we touch everything consciously, because on the Inner Path it is said: Whatever you do, do it totally! That is, do it with awareness, with concentration.

On these two inner days, we touch only what is necessary and eliminate curiosity. This does not mean that we should act unnaturally, but should simply train our sense of touch during its usual activity. For example, we do not have to lean against this or that or prop ourselves up with a table or chair. We can also stand straight, that is, upright.

If we succeed in gaining control over our sense of touch, then everything that we reach for and touch will be done harmoniously. We will not reach for something hastily nor will we apply excessive pressure on objects and things. We will not lean here or there or prop ourselves up here or there. We will come to recognize that whatever is done from within, from our opened spiritual consciousness, becomes harmonious in time. We will then do everything we need to do with ease and grace.

During the two outer days, we give free rein to our sense of touch: We take hold of objects and things more firmly and apply a stronger pressure to them. We touch everything the eye sees and the sense of touch wants to feel in an uncontrolled way. However, here too, we do not want to be fanatic, but let things happen as before, when we were not yet consciously on the Inner Path. Again we record in our mystical journal what we experience during the inner and outer days.

Dear brother, dear sister, record in your mystical journal only what is essential, the important aspects of the inner and outer days. Record what you experience on the outer days with brief notations on the left side of your journal, and what you experience on the inner days, on the right side. There is no time limit for you in doing the exercises, that is, no certain period of time, but you should not do them too often. Some good advice: About once every three weeks, you can live two consecutive days from within and the following two days externally, (that is, the way you lived before the Inner Path).

Dear brother, dear sister, record the following sentence into your mystical journal:

People of the Spirit sit, stand and walk in an upright manner, for their cast of mind, too, is upright.

The following sentences, too, would be an enrichment for us. The one who wants to enter them into his mystical journal can do so:

People of the Spirit do not walk with a bowed head, with their eyes directed solely to the ground, thinking and brooding over the past and the future.

The following sentence is also a pearl, an enrichment, for our mystical journal. It reads:

The more light-filled the soul is, the more upright the person is, since his cast of mind corresponds to his light-filled soul, from which flow positive powers.

*Our sister Gabriele guided us further
along in the spiritual teachings:*

Dear brother, dear sister, now we come to the subject of exaggerated gesticulation. Exaggerated gesticulation also leads us to without, that is, it changes our body rhythm, whereby our nervous system becomes tense.

People of the Spirit are people who live from within and do not use exaggerated gestures while speaking, no matter what the subject of conversation may be. They remain in harmony.

The All-harmony is balanced rhythm and sound. Spiritual and inward-oriented people will accentuate their harmonious speech – which is harmonious sound despite the words – with graceful gestures. This is not gesticulation in the usual sense, but a harmonious communication, which pleasantly colors or accentuates the spiritual language of a refined quality.

People of the Spirit stand and walk, as already mentioned, in an upright manner, just as their inner attitude is. While standing, their arms are not folded and their hands are not constantly moving; instead, arms and hands come into line with the upright posture of the body. The arms hang down harmoniously or the hands rest in one another in back of the body, near the center of Order.

Our spiritual teacher, Brother Emanuel, makes every effort to lead us into becoming true God-people, who ennoble themselves more and more and express the divine, pure and beautiful. This is what he said to us in 1985, and it is as true today as it was then:

Your hands should not be in the pockets of your overcoat or jacket, unless it is very cold and you have no gloves handy.

Gabriele continued:

When our arms hang down loosely and harmoniously and when we walk harmoniously, then the arms begin to move rhythmically. The effect of this posture is that the body straightens automatically. We do not look just at the ground, but also far and wide, to absorb the forces of infinity. The relaxed, rhythmical movements of our arms also give our body more energy. This rhythmic body-mechanism actually leads to increased strength.

Dear brother, dear sister, try it! You should experience on yourself what it means to keep your hands in the pockets of your jacket or overcoat, or to move your arms rhythmically. If we have achieved an upright body posture, then, as mentioned before, our eyes will not be fixed just to the ground, and will not absorb the frequencies that vibrate close to the ground – the heavy, dark thoughts of our fellow men – but will, above all, take in the powers from the universe, because we look into the vast expanses. In the higher spheres, vibrate higher powers!

Our inner attitude has its effect on our sitting and walking posture. An upright sitting posture and an upright way of walking bring about an inner feeling of liberation, a feeling of expanse and a becoming aware of oneself: I am a child of the cosmos.

Brother Emanuel addressed us with "dear friends" and admonished us to ennoble our sense of touch as well as all other senses, so that the grace of our inner being, the grace of the spirit being, can shimmer through our physical body. He also admonishes us to practice walking in the right, that is, upright, way and to practice a well-mannered spiritual movement:

Do not cross your arms and legs, nor support your head with your hands.

Gabriele continued:

This posture indicates pessimism, rejection and carelessness. Crossing arms and legs also indicates a complicated way of thinking, which resembles a maze. Crossed arms and legs also have a corresponding effect on the aura of a person: A careless, leisurely posture encourages and intensifies the pessimism, arrogance and carelessness which may already exist in a person. Such behavior can, in the long run, build up further fields of tension, which can discharge in many different ways, depending on the correspondences that are presently effective in the soul and person.

Dear brother, dear sister, our spiritual teacher, Brother Emanuel, gave us another task in 1985. It will always hold true on the Inner Path, for it, too, contributes to our ennoblement.

The following task is not meant to be done just once. It will serve us again and again, when we cannot overcome our thoughts, worries and difficulties. The students of the level of Order who did this task in 1985 were very enthusiastic about it. They turned to this exercise over and over again when they were unable to overcome something immediately. And now, to the task.

Brother Emanuel said:

Many a one among you is still afflicted with worries, difficulties and problems. As long as you live in the midst of these vibrating complexes, you think they are important and cannot be surrendered to Christ so easily.

For this reason, Brother Emanuel advised us
to do the following exercise:

In sensations, place yourselves into the cosmos, into the middle of the universe. Close your eyes, go within and see yourselves floating or standing in the midst of infinity, of the cosmos. Leave your difficulties and problems on the earth, where you have moved them or where they have their origins. Vibrate upward in your sensations and speak the following highly vibrating words, which shall lend you wings to accomplish your task more easily. Speak these positive powers into your inner being:

> "I am a cosmic being;
> my homeland is the universe,
> the cosmos.
> I vibrate upward,
> toward the suns and worlds of infinity.
> My problems and difficulties remain on earth."

These words should be one with your world of sensations and thoughts; then you will be able to do this task successfully.

Dear brother, dear sister, if in your sensations you are now in the cosmos, then look down on the difficulties and problems you left behind, which have remained attached to the temporal, to matter.

Gabriele:

Only when we stand above our difficulties and problems, do we recognize that they are trivial and unimportant and that we should not attach too much importance to them. When we look at things from the point of view of the universe – that is, when we gain a large distance from our difficulties and problems – we see the unessential and transitory. From there, from the cosmos, we suddenly realize how foolish it is to be preoccupied with unimportant things over and over again.

There in the cosmos, far from our problems and difficulties, we get a sense of the meaning of cosmic consciousness, of what living in unity with the Eternal means. There in the cosmos, we get a sense of what it means to live in unity with all Being.

So when we are able to enter the cosmos, infinity, in our sensations, we feel that we are suns that radiate and shine much brighter than all the countless suns of the totality.

*Gabriele encouraged us
and gave us the following advice:*

Dear brother, dear sister, this task is wonderful. Practice doing it joyfully and you will conquer the base aspects, the difficulties and problems, more quickly.

Brother Emanuel also admonishes us to see the beautiful and good in everything that exists. He said that even in the negative there is the seed of the positive. Look into it consciously and you will see not only the negative but also the positive – and then affirm it! In this way, you will gradually become a positively oriented person.

Life is in all things. Communicate with the positive forces in the bushes that are turning green, in the shrubs and trees, in the blooming flowers, in everything that is. Every season has its beauty. You can find the power of God, the positive, in all things: in the rain, in the snow, in the storm and the wind, in the cold, the warmth and the heat.

Brother Emanuel said:

Do not complain, but accept everything the day brings and see the positive in everything. Then each day will be an eventful, God-lived day for you.

Gabriele:

And so, when we practice seeing the good in all things and communicating with the forces of love, we will consciously be a part of the great whole.

If we are willing to discard our human difficulties, problems and sorrows, we will progress more quickly on the path within, because our five senses, too, refine more quickly, and the antennas, the senses, turn inward, to the core of being of our soul. What then radiates from within to without is the purity of the being, the light-filled soul, the grace of the spirit being.

Dear sister, dear brother, in 1985 our spiritual teacher, Brother Emanuel, asked the brothers and sisters of the level of Order some questions. These questions concern every one of us. He said:

Dear brothers and sisters, I would now like to cautiously approach you with some questions.

I would like to address these questions to the female and male principles, the women and the men, asking them to think about them and to answer them for themselves. I will now cautiously approach the female principles with my questions:

Why do so many women wear long trousers? Is this feminine? Is this beautiful? Why is artificially curled hair necessary? Why the artificial coloring of your hair?

So many people still wear masks. Why must you put on a second mask, which covers up the first one with various pastes and colors? Oh recognize, if the inner grace is enhanced with soft shades, there is no objection to this. But when the first mask has not yet been discarded, a second mask is too mask-like.

For the three-dimensional world, the Spirit makes suitable concessions for very era, insofar as they are consistent with the eternal law. This is why long pants can still be approved of when it is very cold, or in the garden, perhaps at home or when hiking. But why must there be long pants in general, which make our female principles look so austere and masculine?

Dear sisters, I give you these questions to answer. You can talk about them between yourselves. I know very well why I have selected my questions so carefully. I do not want to force you into anything with these questions. The spirit of life just wants to ennoble soul and person.

Dear brothers and sisters, also colors, forms and sounds have their effect upon soul and person. Soft colors and harmonious sounds stimulate the soul as well as the person's disposition.

> Brother Emanuel then spoke to the
> male principles. He said:

I do not want to spare you:

Why do some of you have long hair and a beard? Which idols are you imitating? Or do you want to hide yourselves behind your beard? Then what do you want to be or what do you want to hide?

You are right when you say: "Before the time of Jesus of Nazareth and during His lifetime, men also had beards and long hair." Recognize, my friends, my brothers: Then there were, however, loose flowing robes with few corners or edges. Hair, beard and clothing were one flow. The light, the vibration, refracts on corners and edges.

The many edges and corners on your clothing lead to disharmony. The long hair causes the tips of the hair to come into contact with the corners and edges of the clothing, which charges them with negative energy. The same holds true for the beard. It rubs against the collar of the jacket, the overcoat or the shirt. Besides, nowadays there are suitable tools with accessories which make it possible to quickly shave one's face without a waste of time or great effort.

Dear brothers, I do not want to deprive you of your long hair and beards. I simply want to draw your attention to their effects. I repeat my question: Whom are you imitating? What do you want to hide?

Dear brothers, look at the too tight pants – perhaps dirty, shabby and frayed – that you wear. Is this the grace of the soul or is it the negligence of the person? Is it nice and pleasant to deliberately wear old and ragged clothes? I am also thinking of your pullovers, jackets and the like.

Dear brothers, considering that the outer affects the inner being, what is the effect of such clothing?

As already revealed, I am simply encouraging you to think about it. I do not want to dictate anything to you. Everyone has his free will. But recognize: Forms, colors, sounds and fragrances influence the inner being. The external shapes the inner being and the inner being shapes the outer! When the five senses are turned to the inner being, to the divine, when the soul is light and noble, then the person will dress in an orderly and light way, of course, according to the season.

Brother Emanuel continued: Dear students, neat and clean clothing does not increase our arrogance or craving to be liked. Rather, the person on the path within who dresses neatly brings about humility in his heart.

Recognize, dear brother, dear sister: Nature adorns itself in the most glorious colors and forms to the glory of the All-Highest. Nature gives itself in the fullness, because God is the fullness.

Observe frequently the colors and forms of flowers and leaves, how pure and delicate the blossoms are and how beautifully formed the leaves are, moving gracefully and harmoniously in the wind. The one who observes nature in the unity with God recognizes that everything adorns itself in His honor.

Gabriele:

Our adornment should be our noble and pure thoughts and our fine, harmonious movements. The result will be clean, light and harmonious clothing. For as it is in our inner being, so is our appearance and ultimately our surroundings.

The Spirit of God always advises us to choose the golden mean. This means that all exaggeration is bad. The right measure in all things brings about inner contentment and leads many a one out of grief, sad thoughts and human compulsions.

Our spiritual teacher, Brother Emanuel, revealed to us:

A pretty dress or a clean suit have a positive effect, from without to within. Colors and forms can attract base thoughts; but they can also chase away negative and brooding thoughts. It depends on the form and color of the clothing and how the person reacts to them.

Reactions are different, depending on the mood and inhibition of the individual. Light colors, light fabrics and clean clothing often drive away gloomy and sad thoughts.

A person buys his clothing and dresses himself according to his momentary mood. Bright and light clothes should be worn to brighten up a possibly dark mood. Everything light, pure, clean and bright has a positive effect on a person's world of thoughts. Dark colors and dirty clothing can have the opposite effect.

Gabriele brought the following to our attention:

Every one of us can use these explanations of our spiritual teacher as a mirror for himself.

Brother Emanuel also gave us
some glimpses into our eternal homeland:

Oh do not say that the spiritual world has little understanding, little dynamism!

I will use a word of the world, so that you can understand me. I'll say this word. It is "humor." What man calls "humor" is expressed in the divine world as inner joy, inner dynamism, selflessness and willingness to do everything in honor of the Almighty. Your word "humor" may also be replaced by "joyful, powerful dynamism."

Be of good cheer! It is not so serious in the eternal home, as some of you may think. We, too, adorn ourselves in honor of the Father. All pure Being created by God is beautiful and self-luminous from within – and so is every spirit being. Everything pure is self-luminous. Moreover, the beautiful raiments of the spirit beings and the soft, noble, fine jewelry are indicative of spiritual life; for in the Kingdom of God, the fullness is manifest and accessible to all. Both the male and the female spirit beings wear – as you have already heard – long flowing robes; they also wear delicate jewelry. The robes of the male principles are wide and flowing, those of the female beings are girded with a noble belt.

In the eternal Being, in your home and ours, there are also celebrations of love: The spirit beings come together for harmonious games and gatherings. They create round dances and hear the gentle sounds performed by spirit beings on their instruments.

Gabriele:

Brother Emanuel reminds us that the Inner Path should be a joy. We should conquer our human ego with joy and thankfulness toward God, so that we gain divine power. The Inner Path which is walked successfully brings about inner dynamism and selflessness.

Dear brother, dear sister, Brother Emanuel's words have now strengthened us again. We will walk the Inner Path vivified by the inner joy that Christ, the light of redemption, is so near to us that we may go to meet Him, arrayed with the adornment of virtue and in the certainty that we will not be strangers in the Kingdom of God.

*I would now like to briefly **summarize** the lessons and tasks:*

The sense of touch, dealt with in this lesson, is one of the five senses of man. The previous tasks given to us by our spiritual teacher, Brother Emanuel, served to bring our other four senses under control.

When we now take the five senses as a whole and look at them from the spiritual point of view, we recognize that in many cases the hand wants to touch what the physical eye perceives. The eye wants to see the source of what the nose registers as odors and fragrances. The sense of touch reacts simultaneously: For example, the person reaches for the flask with an aromatic content and brings it to his nose. Or stimulated by the good smells coming from the kitchen, he goes to the stove, lifts the lid off the pot and sticks his nose into it, in order to fully absorb the good smell of the contents.

Another example: A person sees a pretty fabric and walks over to it, so that he can touch it. Or he sees furniture in different forms and colors. He goes to them, in order to touch them, to examine them and think about them. He sees, for instance, the beautiful flowers in the garden, in the fields or the woods. Driven by his senses of sight, smell and touch, he walks toward them, either to touch them or to smell them or even to pick them.

And so, we constantly endeavor to take into our hand or touch what we register. We are also driven by our sense of hearing; driven by curiosity, we become eavesdroppers, listening in on what does not concern us and is, after all, none of our business.

These stirrings and inclinations are human and show that the five senses are turned without. Vehemence and curiosity lead us again and again into the world of the stimulation of the senses. Our uncontrolled senses compel our desires and conceptions. They want to be actualized.

Compulsive desires stimulate us intensely to think of wanting to possess, to be and to have. Envy, animosity and resentment can then come from this, when our neighbor has something we do not have and when we want the same or similar thing.

When the five senses of a person are turned toward the material world, he wants, whenever possible, to see everything, hear everything and to smell pleasant fragrances. He wants to taste good food and drinks and to touch everything within his reach. These human traits of the ego never lead to inner stillness.

Our five senses are at the same time, the five antennas of the person. The five senses, the antennas, are constantly trying to convey to the receiving person every-

thing that lies in him in the way of curiosity, desires and demands. Our five human senses take hold of us and make of us the plaything of earthly forces or of influences from the soul realms.

We are often unknowing subjects without will who let themselves be driven by their unrestrained senses. The game of the senses with the person can lead to further karmic burdens, because the person gives his senses free rein. Thus, he takes in every vibration conveyed to him by his senses. And so, the person will be at the mercy of his senses until he has them under control.

When our consciousness is aligned to such an extent that we can accomplish many things with the power of God – by subjecting our thinking, feeling and willing to the eternal will – then we are protected not only from the stimulation of the senses, but also largely from many unlawful vibrations, as well as from viruses and harmful bacteria, unless they are attracted by a cause that has become effective in the soul and that has the same level of vibration as the virus or bacteria.

Brother Emanuel said in his revelation:

People touch furniture, fabric, clothing and many other objects. They leave their traces, that is, their vibrations, everywhere. All sorts of vibrations are on every material object. Thus, the person who cannot control his sense of touch, since he has not refined his five senses for the most part – because he is still oriented to this side of life and is not All-conscious – absorbs many frequencies that are vibrating on his plane of consciousness.

Gabriele:

And so, dear sister, dear brother, we have heard that our aura absorbs all the vibrations that vibrate at a like rate as the correspondences already in us or in the process of development. The forces we absorb have their effect, in turn, on our world of thoughts.

When one and the same thought is entertained over and over again, a thought-complex grows from this. A thought-complex is more or less a greater or smaller correspondence. A correspondence in the making may lie in the consciousness or in the subconscious.

The correspondence is a magnetic field that attracts everything that vibrates on that wavelength. A correspondence, a thought-complex, is therefore a target for the most differing energy fields – the energy fields in the atmosphere as well as those in the spheres of purification or the energy fields of souls, which vibrate similarly as the thought-complex, the correspondence.

Unlawful forces that influence us cause disorder and tension in the nervous system. They lead to nervousness and may produce illness over the course of time. Positive forces stimulate the nervous system, relax the body and cause the soul and person to come into a higher and finer vibration. For this reason, we should do everything in full awareness! And so, we should think and live in a concentrated way and orient our senses, the antennas, more and more toward the beautiful, noble, good and pure things, toward the divine.

Let me remind you once again of the exercises: We practice the ennoblement of our sense of touch. For two days we live very consciously from within, thus refining our sense of touch. For two days we live as we did up to now, without controlling ourselves. We thereby stimulate our smaller and greater correspondences, which then rise and show us again where we still are in terms of our consciousness. When we do this exercise without fanaticism and only about every three weeks, then only what we can conquer with the help of Christ will rise from our inner being.

During the two inner days, we will touch things or reach for them from within. This will therefore be done harmoniously! We will not reach for things hastily and will not exert excessive pressure on objects and things. Whatever is done from within is harmonious. It happens with ease, agility and buoyancy.

During the two outer days, we reach for things as usual, without thinking, and we exert pressure on objects as we did until now. We touch everything that comes to mind and that the eye perceives and the sense of touch wants to feel. However, we do not go about it fanatically, we let it happen just as it did up to now, when we were not yet aware of our senses.

Dear brother, dear sister, do not forget to record in your mystical journal what you have recognized on the inner days as well as the outer days. You will thus recognize after some time what progress you have made on the Inner Path, because the journal will show what you have overcome and what still needs to be overcome. It will also show your humanness as well as the more subtle aspects already developed in your life.

Also, we should not lean against nor hold on to everything. We should stand and sit upright. You have probably already recorded the following sentence into your journal:

> *People of the Spirit sit, stand and walk upright, since their cast of mind, too, is upright.*

We have learned to pay attention to our body rhythm. With this exercise, we learn that exaggerated gesticulation, too, is a sign of inner unrest, of our still present ego. Harmonious and aligned people will gracefully accentuate their words, in that their gestures – that is, the movement of their hands – will be harmonious while they speak. However, we can also fold our hands together in front of our body, resting one hand in the other, near the center of Order. In this way, we are also upright and can listen to the conversation consciously, that is, without digression of thought.

When we stand upright, the arms hang down relaxed and harmonious; and when we walk, the arms begin to move rhythmically. In this way, our body straightens even more. We will not look only at the ground, but also into the vast expanses grasping the infinite, the power in all Being.

The rhythmic movement of the arms brings about increased energy for the organism. We realize how wonderfully the human being is built and formed and that he has the possibility, with certain rhythmic movements, to direct the life energy to his body from without.

When we are seated, we should not fold our arms or cross our legs, nor support our head with our hands. Brother Emanuel tells us that this posture indicates pessimism, rejection and carelessness. This posture has a disruptive effect on our nervous system and on the energy field of our soul.

Dear sister, dear brother, I would like to remind you of another task regarding our difficulties and problems. As long as we are in the midst of our difficulties, we think that we cannot simply give them over to Christ to be dissolved. Therefore, I would like to briefly mention again the exercise Brother Emanuel gave us:

In our sensations, we should place ourselves into the cosmos, into the center of the universe. Thus, we should feel as though we are floating or standing in the middle of the universe, while leaving our difficulties and problems here on earth. While doing this, we close our eyes and, with the following words that we speak into our inner being, we can free ourselves more easily from our difficulties and problems. I repeat these brief sentences:

> *"I am a cosmic being.*
> *My homeland is the universe,*
> *the All.*
> *I vibrate upward,*
> *toward the suns and worlds of infinity.*
> *My problems and difficulties remain on earth."*

When we say these sentences, we should give life to every word with our sensations and thoughts. And so, in our sensations and thoughts we should be with our words, with what we express. Then, we will receive the strength to stand above our difficulties and problems and to look at them in the right way.

When we can place ourselves into the cosmos in our sensations, we will look down on our difficulties and problems, which stayed behind here in the world, in the temporal. From a certain distance, we realize that many things that preoccupy us daily are trivial and unimportant.

From there, from the cosmos, we suddenly recognize how foolish it is to preoccupy ourselves again and again with unimportant things.

Far from our problems and difficulties, we sense what cosmic consciousness means. We also sense what unity with all Being means.

Dear brother, dear sister, reflect also on what our spirit teacher, Brother Emanuel, revealed about our external appearance, about our hair and beard, the artificial coloring of our hair and about our "mask," by which he means the ego, and behind which we hide our thoughts.

Think about your clothes as well, about their color and shape. Everything is energy. Color, form and sound affect us. They stimulate us or cause depression or aggression, according to what is in us. And do not forget to contemplate the harmonies and symphonies of nature and include yourself – the being of God – in the symphonies and harmonies, in the colors and forms of nature.

At the end of the lessons on the level of Order, our sister Gabriele spoke words of spiritual encouragement to us:

Dear brother, dear sister, the Inner Path is the path of love. We brothers and sisters in Universal Life walk it with you. We, too, have our difficulties and problems, which we will master with the help of Christ. You are not alone on the Inner Path, not even when you are there and we are here. The person who loves God and his neighbor is linked with everyone, no matter where he may live.

True life knows no boundaries; it is without time or space. True love links from place to place, from eon to eon; it is timeless, eternally flowing. We want to enter into this stream. We extend our hands to one another and support each other. God helps us to progress, to again reach the origin of the source.

Those of like mind, all those who are struggling along with you to become free from their human ego, wish you the unity with them and the peace of the heavens.

Greetings in God, dear brother, dear sister!

Peace,

Gabriele

Self-examination for Proceeding to the Level of Will

Brother Emanuel, our spiritual teacher, revealed:

The one who has brought his thoughts under control for the most part on the level of Order was able to and can mostly prevail over his senses.

The one who could and can curb his speech as a result of the schooling on the level of Order is already a small master of his ego.

The one who was able to leave the past behind, everything that preoccupied his person again and again and was able to give it over to the Eternal has truly grown and is ready to step onto the level of Will.

Dear brother, dear sister, if you have conscientiously and daily carried out the tasks and exercises given in this book, you probably succeeded in establishing order for the most part in your world of thoughts and sensations and in your life.

If you now want to step onto the next level, the level of Will, you may examine yourself with the help of the following questions, as to whether you have already laid the necessary foundation for it on the level of Order.

On the level of Order, were you able to:
– *control your thoughts,*
– *curb your speech and*
– *master your senses for the most part?*

Only the one who loves God, his Father, more than this world – and more than himself, than his thinking and wanting – can put his thoughts in order and orient them toward the spiritual goal, God.

The person who still makes considerable worldly demands for himself, that is, who lets his thoughts circle around his own interests, in that he still wants to possess this or that and still wants to be this or that, does not yet have his heart free for the Inner Path.

Have you managed to clear up your past, and is it merely a memory in your consciousness?

The one who lives in his past cannot master what comes toward him every day. He will then not gain mastery over his life, but will be subject to his human ego.

Did you manage to mostly give over your egotistical aspects, your "I, my and me"?

Only then can you learn concentration in order to hold your own on the level of Will.

On the level of Will, you will learn more and more to recognize and master yourself. You will thus become more sensitive and permeable for the spiritual powers. Your conscience will react more intensely, because the light of Christ becomes brighter in you on the level of Will.

The one who walks the path of love conscientiously will very soon realize and feel what his wanting, his will, that is, his personal will, is, and what the divine will, the impersonal will, is.

In the schooling of the level of Will, a person's wanting should be surrendered more and more to the Eternal.

It is not we who act, but it is God who acts through us. We thus learn the right concentration in accordance with the spirit of divine will.

Glossary of Spiritual Terms

Absolute Law: *The Absolute Law is what is absolutely pure from which only the pure emerges and into which only the pure can enter. It is the aura of the heavenly worlds (*heaven), the breath of God in which all that is pure moves (*ether, *Holy Spirit). The Absolute Law is the life. Everything outside the Absolute Law is expiation in the *causal law, in the law of sowing and reaping.*

Absoluteness: *The pure, eternal divine Being, the eternity; the *heavens, the eternal home; the eternal life, the law of God (*Absolute Law)*

Actualization: *Putting into practice those aspects of the divine law which I have recognized, and a consistent life in accordance with the divine law. Constant actualization leads to the step-by-step fulfillment of the divine laws. Only actualization and fulfillment result in the unfoldment of the *consciousness. The enlightened person lives in the fulfillment of the eternal laws (*Absolute Law). He draws from the divine wisdom, which is effective in him.*

All-Spirit: *The Holy Spirit; the eternally flowing, all-permeating and maintaining *ether; see: *God; *primordial power.*

Angel: **Spirit being, *cherub, *seraph*

Astral planes: *The astral planes are the four lower levels of the seven *Fall-planes; they are spheres of purification (*planes of purification) for *souls. In the astral planes, the causal law, the law of cause and effect, holds true: Via cause and effect, the eternal Spirit leads to recognition and turning back.*

The souls in the astral planes are subject to the gravitation of the earth (and to the influence of the planets) and thus are in the wheel of rebirth (*reincarnation).

The person who seeks and maintains contact with astral forces or souls practises occultism or spiritism, thus exposing himself to the dangers connected with this (being drained of strength, being influenced and so on).

Atoms (spiritual): *They are the components of all forms in infinity. The spiritual *ether, the life force, consists of spiritual atoms. The spiritual atom consists of the atomic nucleus, the so-called *core of being (in it there is an interaction between the two particles, negative and positive), the three *attributes of God and the four *natures of God, that is, the seven basic powers of creation, which are effective in seven elliptical orbits around the nucleus. *atom-types, spiritual.*

Atom-types, spiritual: *There are five spiritual types of atoms:*

ether atoms – they correspond to the three *attributes (powers) of God;

development (motion) atoms – they correspond to the *nature (power) of divine Earnestness;

Creation (formation) atoms – they correspond to the *nature (power) of divine Wisdom;

Carrier (stabilisation) atoms – they correspond to the *nature (power) of divine Will;

fertility atoms – they correspond to the *nature (power) of divine Order.

Attributes of God: *The three attributes of God, together with the four *natures of God, form the seven basic powers of creation. The attributes of God are called patience, love and mercy. In contrast to the *nature beings, these powers are developed in the children of God, the pure *spirit beings. For this reason, the attributes of God are also called attributes of *filiation.*

Aura: *Energy-radiation of all living beings, visible to some people; portrayed as a "halo" in the arts; it shows the momentary condition of the *soul of the person, his frame of mind, development and character.*

Body movements: **consciousness exercises*

Body rhythm: The body rhythm is the movement of all spiritual and material bodies. In reference to man, the movement of the *spirit body and of the physical body.

Brother Emanuel: Brother Emanuel is the *cherub of divine Wisdom. He is the responsible servant in the Work of Redemption of the Lord and teaches mankind the *Inner Path in the *Mystical School of Christ through the *prophetic word (*teaching prophet).

Castigation: The repressing and suppressing of human desires, longings, faults and weaknesses. It does not lead to freedom but, among other things, to intolerance, *fanaticism and to stagnation on the *Inner Path. Instead, we should recognize our humanness and should overcome it with the help of the power of *Christ, by examining and controlling our experiences, by refining and ennobling ourselves step by step, by affirming, that is, by strengthening that which is spiritually higher – through proper discipline.

Causal law: The law of cause and effect, the law of karma: "Whatever you sow, you shall reap." The divine law for the earth and the *planes of purification. Because the Divine can no longer guide the heavily burdened human beings and *souls directly (*inner word), it guides them indirectly through the *causal law.

Cherub: *A cherub is a male law angel (*spirit being) which was directly created by God at the beginning of creation; it is also called archangel. There are seven cherubs, each of them representing a *nature or attributes of God. Together with its *dual, a *seraph, the cherub governs the heavenly plane which corresponds to its mentality. Cherub and seraph form a princely couple in heaven.*

Christ: *The first-beheld and firstborn Son of *God-Father; the *Co-Regent of the heavens; He is the Redeemer of mankind through His sacrifice. Since then, every *soul possesses the so-called Redeemer-spark, the supporting, maintaining and home-leading power in every soul.*

Communications: *The energetic processes flowing between senders and receivers (for example, between *programs).*

Conscious mind: *The consciousness of the human mind, thinking, and remembering – our ordinary consciousness.*

Consciousness: *1. The Spirit of God (*ether) in everything that is; the Spirit of God, the *Logos, the *I Am. The one who has opened the first four levels of consciousness in himself immerses more and more into the consciousness of God (*Absolute Law), from*

where he receives pure impulses from the Spirit of God (*inner word).
2. The human consciousness, consisting of *consciousness and subconscious.

Consciousness centers: *The seven consciousness centers in the human being are the control centers for the spiritual energies for the physical body. They direct the spirit power (*ether) to the organs and cells of the body. They correspond to the seven *soul garments. In the eastern religions, they are called "chakras."*

Consciousness exercises: *Body movements inspired by the Spirit of God in Universal Life, accompanied by harmonious music. They are carried out especially before the contemplations of the two Original Christian Development of Consciousness courses. They help to harmonize body and *soul, thus increasing the receptiveness for the spiritual forces of life and healing. Consciousness exercises can also be carried out freely, as one feels.*

Co-Regent of the heavens: **Christ, the first-beheld and firstborn Son of *God-Father, received as heritage the *part-power of the *primordial power. Thus, He is the Co-Regent of the *heavens; He sits on the right of the Father.*

Core of being: *1. Core of being of the ether body of the pure *spirit being and thus the core of being of the *soul, too; its spiritual "heart," the incorruptible spark of God in the innermost being. Each being is linked through this core of being to the great energy cycle of infinity, thus standing in an inseparable connection with *God. Through the core of being, the pure spirit power (*ether) flows into the ether body. In the beings of the fall, it flows from the ether body into the physical body.*

2. Nucleus of the Primordial Central Sun: It consists of two thirds positive and one third negative *primordial power, whose interaction produces the energy for the whole of infinity.

3. Nucleus of the spiritual *atoms: The nucleus of the atom consists in turn of two-thirds positive and one third negative primordial power, whose interaction maintains the energy flow within the *spiritual atom.

Correspondence: *Shadow in the *soul garments, a guilt (wrong behavior) which has not been cleared up. A correspondence becomes especially active (begins to vibrate) when we discover the same or something similar in our neighbor. We can recognize ourselves in our emotions and aggressions (mirror-effect of our neighbor). A correspondence which has been overcome becomes a memory (an experience).*

Deathspan: *The span of time within which the death of the physical body can take place (*lifespan).*

Deed of Redemption: *Due to the constant violations of the divine laws, the *souls became more and more shadowed, that is, the spiritual *atoms rotated more and more slowly and were finally at the point of tipping. This would have meant the degeneration of the souls via the animal, plant, and mineral kingdoms, all the way to the dissolution in the flowing *ether. When Jesus the Christ, said on Calvary: "It is finished!," He withdrew His divine heritage from the *Primordial Central Sun and divided it into sparks. He implanted such a *Redeemer-spark into every soul. This spark maintains the filiation, that is, it prevents a further degeneration of the souls. The Redeemer-spark is the supporting and nourishing power in every soul, the Redeemer-flame in us, in which we can put all faults and weaknesses, which will be dissolved according to His will, if we strive not to sin any longer. See: *Inner Physician and Healer.*

Dual: *A dual is the life partner, the spouse of a pure *spirit being. A male angel (positive principle) and a female angel (negative principle) who join in "matrimony," form a dual couple. They work together in absolute unity. Spiritual children then come into being through *spiritual procreation.*

Ether (spiritual): *The All-Spirit, the universal Spirit, the spiritual primordial energy, the impersonal *God; the Creator-Spirit; the absolute, incorruptible life; the omnipresent power; the *the Logos, the *consciousness in everything that is; the law; the *Holy Spirit, the *breath of God, the od-power, the *love; the primordial power, the eternally flowing, divine life force, the light.*

The ether streams unceasingly from the *Primordial Central Sun. It permeates all Being. It is the substance of everything that is; it vivifies and maintains all pure forms of life and also the material structures; it is the consciousness, the life, in all Being (*matter).

Ether body: *1. The spiritual, that is, the fine-material body of the *spirit beings (angels). It consists of spiritual particles; they can be compared with our coarse-material cells. The "heart" of the ether body is the *core of being ("spark of God"); it receives the divine *ether and conveys this ether to the spiritual particles via the seven centers. Since the ether body is completely irradiated by the divine light-ether – the spirit being lives in the *Absolute Law of God – the ether body is self-luminous.*

2. Ether body in the human being: *soul; shadowed spiritual body in the human being, consisting of the incorruptible *core of being, the spark of God, and the seven burdened garments (*soul garments), from *which the so-called ether tree with the seven *consciousness centers forms. Through these centers of consciousness, the divine energy flows to the organs and cells of the material body.*

Ether chronicle: *A spiritual layer in the finest sphere of the earth's atmosphere – thus, also called atmospheric chronicle; everything is stored in it, everything that was ever thought and done on earth, all opinions and conceptions, that is, true and false things, thus *mixed knowledge.*
People with mediumistic qualities who are not aligned with the absolute and pure source of truth, the Spirit of God, can call up knowledge from the ether chronicle which may contain true and false information.

Ether forms: *The ether forms come forth from the pure *ether. The pure spiritual forms of the *heavens are manifested ether. All these heavenly forms of being are in absolute harmony with the flowing ether.*
The ether forms of the heavens go through a process of development (evolution): from the forms of the heavenly mineral, plant and animal kingdoms, to the forms of the spiritual elemental beings (*nature beings), all the way to the highest form of the pure *spirit beings (angels, in the image of God).

Fall-planes: *The seven spheres of the beyond, outside the pure *heavens. They are separated from the pure heavens by the *light wall. Since the Redeemer-deed* *of Jesus, the Christ, they have become the four *planes of purification (formerly satanic hierarchies, *astral planes) and the three *planes of preparation for the *absoluteness. They correspond to the successive shadowing of the individual *atributes and natures of God in the formerly pure spirit body (*ether body) of the angels (*spirit beings).*

Fanaticism: *To be bound to conceptions; lack of freedom; the person circles around himself and excludes himself from a true community since he is incapable of true tolerance, understanding and selfless love.*

Filiation: *The child's relationship to the Father, the Father-child relationship.*

God: **Holy Spirit, *All-Spirit, *Ether (impersonal God), *God-Father and God-Son, *Christ.*

God-Father: *God-Father is the first and highest form, the manifestation of the *All-Spirit; therefore He is also called Primordial Father (Father-Ur). He is active in all His *attributes and *natures in the omnipresence. He is in absolute unity with the All-Spirit. Together with *Christ, His first-beheld and firstborn Son, He reigns over all of infinity in absolute *love. Every pure *spirit being sees God-Father face to face.*

God-Son: **Christ*

Guardian spirit: *A guardian spirit is a *spirit being (angel) or a largely purified soul from the *planes of preparation to absoluteness. A guardian spirit is put beside every human being and every *soul for guidance and protection.*

Guilt (of the soul): **Karma*

Heaven: *The eternal, pure, divine worlds; the absolute Being. There are seven basic heavens, which correspond to the divine *attributes and *natures. These basic heavens in turn each consist of seven subspheres, since each attribute or nature of God contains each of the others in itself.*

Heroic sacrificial courage: *The consistent decision to give up baseness (humanness) for higher things (divine things), to do what is lawful. The absolute alignment with the divine. To always get up again and again when we have fallen. The motive for heroic sacrificial courage is the love and longing for *God.*

Holy Spirit: *God is spirit, the *All-Spirit (*Ether) which comes forth from the *Primordial Central Sun, from the eternal spiritual energy field, which streams through, vivifies and maintains everything.*

I Am (the): *The I Am is the eternal all-law, the eternal Spirit, the infinite love and the infinity. It is the life* *force in all Being and the Being. The I Am is the impersonal, the selfless, the eternally giving – God. The I Am is the eternal truth, the creative, the law that has taken on form, the spirit being in God.*

Incarnation: *Embodiment that is, encasing, of a *soul in a physical body. Also used for the life on earth of the soul.*

The meaning and purpose of an incarnation is to purge and purify oneself in the power of *Christ step by step – through self-recognition and actualization, through a life in accordance with the divine laws – in order to free oneself from the wheel of rebirth (*reincarnation), thus growing from the *causal law into the *Absolute Law. Some souls incarnate to help others in their development.

Inner Path (in Universal Life): *The path to *God in the innermost part of the *soul, also called mystical path; the path back to the eternal heavenly home (*heaven); the path of the purging and purification of soul and person with the help and guidance of the power of Christ in the person (*Redeemer-power); the path of self-recognition, actualization and fulfilment of the eternal laws of life and of *love. The seven levels of development of the consciousness have to be unfolded successively.*

The Inner Path to God is taught today in all its levels and details by *Christ through His *prophetic word *in the Christian *Mystery School, the high schooling of the Spirit of God. The aim of the Inner Path is that our consciousness become one with *God – to unfold again the divine within the person.*

Inner Physician and Healer: *The divine healing power in man, the Christ-power (*Redeemer spark), is the redeeming and healing power in every *soul. If we are willing to lead our life in accordance with the laws of *love and of life, thus changing our ways – and to entrust ourselves to the Christ-power – then we can receive relief and healing, first for our soul and then, according to His will, for our body as well.*

Inner word: *When the first four levels of consciousness (*natures of God) are purified for the most part on the *Inner Path, *Christ is able to guide His pupils directly, be it through the purified sensations from the *consciousness or through His inner word which can be heard in the innermost being of the person as clearly and distinctly as the human words with the physical ears. The inner word is meant solely for the pupil, personally, not for a second or third person, in contrast to the *prophetic word.*

Intellect: *Human intellectual thinking which is marked by opinions and conceptions, desires and inclinations; it analyzes, aggrandizes and belittles. The intellect is useful at the beginning of the *Inner Path, but in the* *course of time it will be ennobled, refined and inwardly directed. Intellectual thinking will change into "heart-thinking," which streams from the largely developing inner consciousness (*inner word).*

Karma: *Soul guilt. After a *time of grace, a violation (negative cause) of one of the eternal laws through feeling, thinking and acting first enters into the *soul (book of life) by way of the *subconscious and is stored there in one of the seven soul garments as energy, that is, as vibration. Karma is a burden of the soul, which prevents it from being totally irradiated by the divine light-power (*ether); the soul is thus "shadowed." It shows *correspondences.*

The karma can be removed, that is, eliminated, by the divine law of grace, by recognizing the causes, repenting, asking for forgiveness, forgiving and being forgiven by the one who was harmed, and by making amends. To be free from karma means to be free from the wheel of rebirth (*reincarnation). If the karma is not paid off, it comes into effect in the form of physical suffering, illness, need, blows of fate and the like (*causal law).

Lifespan: *The amount of time foreseen for the incarnation of a soul, in which it is to fulfil its life programs (*programs). The lifespan is followed by the *deathspan of the person.*

Light wall: *A radiation wall which separates the pure heavenly worlds (*heavens) from the *Fall-worlds. The light wall contains the light that was left behind by the *spirit beings which left the pure heavens. Only those who acknowledge *Christ as the *Co-Regent of the heavens can pass through the radiation wall back into the *absoluteness, for nobody comes to the Father but through Christ!*

Logos: *The divine *consciousness, the eternal intelligence, "the word," the primordial sensation, the *Absolute Law, the *I Am.*

Love, divine: *The law of infinity; the impersonal, selflessly giving, forever flowing, linking and unifying power of *God; the all-encompassing principle of the divine.*

Mask: *The external "shine" or illusion behind which the person wants to hide his base human emotions, sensations and thoughts.*

Matter: *Ether which has been transformed down as a result of the Fall-event (*Fall-planes); coarse-material form of being; the life on matter which is part of the development plane of Order is limited to the three dimensions and to time and space. The material structures are respirated, vivified and maintained by the *Spirit of God.*

Mentality, spiritual: *A specific *attribute or *nature of God predominates in each *spirit being; it also corresponds to the heavenly plane from which it originated. The specific imprinting of the divine powers in a spirit being form its mentality.*

Messenger of God: *A messenger of God is a *teaching prophet who draws directly from the primordial source, the divine, through his fully developed consciousness – unlike a *revelation – thus interpreting the eternal truth, the *Absolute Law, in his human language. Gabriele of Würzburg is the messenger of God for the end-time.*

Mixed knowledge: *Spiritual knowledge which is still mixed with human conceptions and opinions. If the receiver has self-willed aspirations or is still caught up in his humanness, he calls up information from the atmospheric chronicle (*ether chronicle) or from another astral sender (*astral planes). Hence each person is responsible for every word he passes on to others.*

Mystery School (Christian): *Today *Christ reveals to mankind the direct path to *God through the *prophetic word (*prophet). He teaches the *Inner Path, the Christian mystical path of love, in all detail. The *cherub of divine Wisdom, called *Brother Emanuel on earth, is responsible for this. The path to God in* *the mystical school of Christ begins with a meditative preparatory path and with a meditative path of address, then goes, by way of the intensive schooling, to the seven-fold mystical path – under the direct and immediate, personal guidance of *Christ in the inner being of the person.*

Mystical journal: *The journal of the student in the intensive schooling, in which he writes down his positive and negative experiences, what has been recognized, what still has to be worked on and what has already been overcome – the experiences and insights of the *Inner Path.*

Nature being: *Fine-material spiritual life form in which the natures of God —Order, Will, Wisdom and Earnestness – are fully developed. In the spiritual evolution of the *heavens, the nature beings are the preliminary step to becoming a *spirit being.*

Natures of God: *The natures of God are four of the seven basic creative powers. They are called: Order, Will, Wisdom and Earnestness (*attributes of God).*

Part-power (of the primordial power): *A third of the positive primordial power, the heritage of Christ. *Christ is active in this power in the four *natures of God in the omnipresence. This makes Him the *Co-Regent of infinity.*

With His redemptive deed, Christ divided His heritage into individual sparks; such a Redeemer-spark implanted itself into every *soul. It is the supporting and nourishing power in every soul, which one day will help every soul to return to *absoluteness; for the part-power strives to enter into the primordial power again.

Past: *Everything already past, which can no longer be changed by us, but occupies our thoughts again and again; thus, we do not let go of it, but intensify it with new thought energy. Also the experiences which have not yet been overcome and therefore are still active.*

Planes of preparation: *The three *Fall-planes nearest to the *light wall; they became planes of preparation through the *Redeemer-deed of Jesus Christ.*

Planes of purification: *After the Redeemer-deed of Jesus *Christ, the *astral planes became planes of purification for the *souls.*

Primordial Central Sun: *The heart of the cosmos; the central primordial star of the *heavens, a power field with an infinite power-potential, the source of the *primordial power, of the flowing ether. All energies of infinity stream from the Primordial Central Sun. The seven secondary primordial suns, the prism suns, with the seven heavenly planes, orbit around the Primordial Central Sun.*

Primordial power: *The *All-Spirit (*Holy Spirit), consisting of two thirds positive and one third negative power, which are in interaction – through which energy is produced (*ether).*

Proclaiming prophet: *Unlike *teaching prophets, there have always been proclaiming prophets. Through them, God kept in contact with His children on earth. Through them, He helps mankind to grasp the spiritual knowledge that has already been revealed (*prophet).*

Programs: *Energy-complexes formed by recurring negative sensations, thoughts, words and actions which are stored in the soul garments. Programs serving our earthly life and programs coming from our predispositions and abilities lie in our genes, in our *consciounesss and our subconscious.*
Active programs send and receive. The energetic processes that stream between individual programs are *communications.

Prophet: *A mouthpiece of *God; God speaks (reveals) through the prophet in His divine *I Am. A person with the mission of passing on the divine word to a mankind that is spiritually deaf and blind. The prophet first has to walk the path of purging for soul and person, in order to purify himself for his task. Prophets have always been inconvenient to their contem-*

poraries, because through them God shook them up and admonished them to change their ways. Many prophets were persecuted and killed. The *teaching prophetess of God in our time (the end-time) is Gabriele of Würzburg.

Prophetic word: **Prophet; *inner word; *teaching prophet, *proclaiming prophet.*

Purification planes: **planes of purification*

Redeemer-spark: **Spark of Redemption*

Redeemer-deed of Jesus Christ: **Deed of Redemption*

Reincarnation: *Repeated embodiment (*incarnation) of the *soul, re-embodiment of the soul in a human being. The wheel of rebirth is the alternating presence of the soul: on earth, in the soul-realms, again on earth, etc.*
The person who has grown beyond the first four levels of spiritual development (Order, Will, Wisdom, Earnestness) leaves the field of attraction of the material world; he moves out of the wheel of rebirth and thus out of the effective range of the *causal law. He then lives in the *Absolute Law.

Revelation: *Message from *God through the *inner word in a person as well as through the *prophetic word (*prophet).*

Satana: *Satana is the first female angel (*spirit being) created by God-Father. The Father raised her to be His *dual, and she conceived *Christ as the first-beheld and first-born Son of God-Father. She sat at His left side until negative sensations rose in her; she wanted a separate kingdom and enticed other spirit beings away from obedience God, thus initiating the Fall-event (*Fall-planes of the fall). Satana's ultimate aim was the dissolution of all forms in the eternal *ether. However, this was prevented by the Redeemer-deed of Jesus Christ. She recognized and repented her wrong behaviour and since then has been striving to help all burdened *souls to return to *absoluteness (*heaven). Satana will remain outside the *light wall until every soul has returned.*

Seraph: *The first female angels (*spirit beings) are (except *Satana) the seraphs. The seraphs are the *duals of the *cherubs. Together with them they form the seven heavenly princely couples which preside over the seven heavens; they each represent one *attribute or *nature of God.*

Silver cord: *Silver string, odic cord; spiritual, energetic, flexible and infinitely extendable cord of condensed *ether (odic-) power. When the *soul of a person leaves its body at night, it remains connected with the body through this silver cord. Energy and information flow by way of this connection. When this cord is severed, physical death occurs.*

Soul: *The soul is the burdened *ether body of the once pure *spirit being. It has so-called *soul garments consisting of the shadows which formed as a result of unlawful sensations, thoughts, words and actions. During its incarnation, the soul is in a human body to purge itself in time and space through self-recognition, with the help of the divine power of Christ (*Redeemer-spark). After discarding the physical body, it enters those soul realms (*Fall-planes) which correspond to its spiritual development, that is, to the nature and degree of its burdens, its shadows.*

Everything that we have thought, said and done in this life or in other earthly lives is registered and stored in the soul. The soul is the "book of life."

The pure spirit being, that is, the unburdened *ether body with the so-called *core of being or the spark of God spark in its innermost being – our actual being – lives eternally.

The Redeemer-deed of Christ ensures that each soul will purify itself and again return to the heavenly worlds as a pure spirit being.

Soul guilt: **Karma*

Soul garments: *The soul garments formed when the once pure *spirit being fell into deeper and deeper zones of vibration outside the heavens.*

The seven immaterial soul garments are the lower-vibrating shadows of a pure spirit body. The vio-

lations of the divine law which have not yet been atoned for are stored in them as *correspondences, as debt (*karma). But also the paid off causes rest here as experience, as memory. During *incarnation, the soul garments fold into each other in the human body and out of them develop the *consciousness centers, which are the connecting centers of energy between *soul and person.

Soul particles: *Just as the human body consists of cells, the pure spirit body (*ether body) consists of particles. The structure of the soul can be compared with the overlapping scales of a fish.*
When the particles of the spirit body are shadowed, the spiritual *atoms in the particles are no longer exactly aligned with the source of the life force, the divine *core of being in the innermost of the soul. For this reason the spirit power (*ether), the life force, cannot flow freely in these areas of the soul. Through a life in accordance with the divine laws, the spiritual atoms gradually align again with the core of being, with the *primordial power. The All-Spirit then irradiates increasingly the soul and the person, which leads to the expansion of the *consciousness and the decrease of the soul garments.

Spark of Redemption: *When *Christ said on Calvary: "It is finished!," the divine heritage of Christ, the *part-power of the primordial power, divided into* *individual sparks, whereby such a Christ-spark implanted itself into every soul. This Redeemer-spark, also called Redeemer-light, prevents the soul from declining further toward the dissolution in the eternal *ether. It is the supporting and redeeming power in each soul, the motive force for the return to the Father.*

Spirit: **Holy Spirit, *ether (spiritual)*

Spirit being: *A spirit being (angel) is a child of God and the image of * God-Father; a perfect, free and light-filled being which lives in the pure *heavens, in divine unity and *love. It has developed all the divine *natures and (filiation) *attributes within itself. The highest, most luminous spirit beings are *God-Father and His Son, *Christ. The *cherubs and *seraphs, too, are spirit beings as well as all other angels.*

Spirit body: **Ether body*

Spirit power: **Ether (spiritual)*

Spiritual atom: **Atom (spritual)*

Spiritual procreation: *In the pure love-radiation of a *dual couple of the *heavens (spiritual man = positive principle, spiritual woman – negative principle),* *a nature being develops in a spiritual cocoon into a perfect *spirit being, through the unfoldment of the divine filiation-attributes: patience, love, mercy (*attributes of God).*

Subcommunication: *Subcommunications are communications of programs lying in the subconscous and in the soul garments. By way of these subcommunications, the person can be controlled by outside forces. It is necessary to recognize and eliminate these subcommunications.*

Subconscious: *The subconscious lies in the deeper layers of the brain; it stores things that have been forgotten, not overcome and repressed in this life. Through the *Inner Path, one becomes aware again of many things and can work on and dissolve them.*

Teaching prophet: *Teaching prophets are great *prophets who appeared and appear in times of radical change in the history of mankind. Through the teaching prophets, God reveals to mankind aspects of the divine truth, of the divine law (*Absolute Law), thus far unknown; in particular, the details (levels) of the *Inner Path to God which the teaching prophets have walked ahead of their fellow men. When the teaching prophet can draw directly from the very source (the divine) as a result of having fully unfolded his consciousness, he becomes a *messenger of God.*

Gabriele of Würzburg is the teaching prophetess of God for the end-time.

Thought-complex: *Our thoughts are energy forms, which accompany us as well as influence us as well as like-minded or similarly-minded people, if we are open to them. The more often and intensively we think something, wish for something, etc., the stronger and greater the thought-energy complex becomes. According to the law "like attracts like", we attract the same or similar energy fields – also from the atmospheric chronicle (*ether chronicle) – or earth-bound *souls. Thought-complexes dissolve when we forgive and ask for forgiveness, when we begin to think and live consciously and positively.*

Time of Grace: *When a person has set a negative cause through unlawful sensations, thoughts or actions (*karma), it will first enter the *aura of the person. Now the person has the chance to realize he did something wrong, to repent, to ask for forgiveness, to forgive and to make amends. During this time of grace, he receives divine impulses more often via his conscience. If the person recognizes his mistake and turns back, changes his ways, the negative cause can dissolve. But if he does not turn back, that is, if he lets the time of grace run out, the negative cause will enter the *soul and become a burden of the soul, a soul*

guilt (*karma) which strives to bring out a corresponding effect (*causal law) sooner or later.
The more we advance on the *Inner Path, the shorter the time of grace becomes, that is, the quicker a cause enters the soul and the sooner it brings about an effect.

World: *By "world" (or "worldly"), the revealing Spirit of God does not mean the planet earth, but everything that has emerged on this earth as a result of the unlawful activity of mankind.*

Universal Life Book Series

This Is My Word. A and Ω
*The Gospel of Jesus
The Christ-Revelation
which the world does not know*
1074 pages / Order No. S 007en

*The Great Cosmic Teachings
of JESUS of Nazareth*
*to His Apostles and Disciples
who could understand them*

*With explanations by Gabriele
in the Great Teaching Church of the Spirit of God*
Vol. I, 255 pages / Order No. S 317en

*Live the Moment –
and You Will See and Recognize Yourself*
76 pages / Order No. S 315en

Where Did I Come From? Where Am I Going?
75 pages / Order No. S 407en

*Healing by Faith –
The Holistic Healing*
97 pages / Order No. S 330en

Are You Who You Think You Are?
55 pages / Order No. S 332en,
includes music for contemplation

God Heals
64 pages / Order No. S 309en

Me, Me, Me
The Spider in the Web
The Law of Correspondence and the Law of Projection
212 pages / Order No. S 325en

Father-Words for You, too
111 pages / Order No. S 108en

Inner Prayer
Heart Prayer, Soul Prayer, Ether Prayer,
Healing Prayer
128 pages / Order No. S 307en

To order any of these books or to obtain a complete catalog of all our books, please contact:

Verlag DAS WORT GmbH
Max-Braun-Straße 2
97828 Marktheidenfeld-Altfeld
Germany
or:
Universal Life, the Inner Religion
PO Box 3549
Woodbridge, CT 06525
U S A
1-800-846-2691
www.universal-spirit.cc
e-mail: info@universelles-leben.org